MW01242826

FALLING TOWARDS HEAVEN

DANIEL MCGHEE

Authors Note: The events in this story are all true as far as my memory and perception of them have interpreted. Names and minor details have been changed to protect the rights of those involved. It is not my wish to include anyone else unwillingly in my tale of transparency. We are all at different stages of our own journeys.

The Library of Congress has catalogued the paperback edition as follows:
Phoenix Rising Publishing:
McGhee, Daniel. 2022
Falling Towards Heaven/Daniel McGhee
Library of Congress control number: 2022935273

ISBN 978-1-7339485-1-7
ISBN 978-1-7339485-2-4

Published by Phoenix Rising Publishing

www.chasingaflawedsun.com

This book is dedicated to Bethany, Corrine, my wife Alisha and all the angels that I met along the way that loved me when I didn't have the self awareness to love myself.

"Flying is learning how to throw yourself at the ground and miss."

—Douglas Adams

The fall is eternal.
It is here that we must change our perception.
By changing our perception we reverse gravity.
It is our duty to soar.
We owe it to ourselves.

PREFACE

THE MIRROR ALWAYS told me lies. It scolded me when I expected it to solve me. I always walked away from it more withered than I appeared. This time as I stood transfixed in the disappointment of my reflection, I heard her voice behind me, also scolding.

"You've always been imprisoned in your own body, and it's annoying."

It awakened me like the first drop of icy rain on a sleeping man's face. It was truth. The truth will snap you out of a walking coma faster than any attempt at enlightenment. I had been trapped. It was the only way I knew how to feel. I had been swimming through the garbage of self-doubt for so long that I knew nothing else.

Her lips spoke softly just behind my ear, "Well then, let me teach you how to fly."

I exhaled the last of the smoke from my lungs forcefully at the dull reflection before me. I stubbed the rest of the smoldering cigarette into the glass ashtray and fell backwards into her invisible embrace.

Her voice came through in waves. Her words painted

faint streaks on the horizon of my drifting mind. My soul freely traveled from one acting debut to the next as my dreams blended like watercolors into one another. The sounds in the hospital room played a symphony in the backdrop of each dream, each with their own place and time until their realities began to blend into my actual one. Suddenly the beeps and hums of the machines became exactly what they were, and my soul returned to its earthly vessel. I stirred myself awake in the dark room.

Her voice came from somewhere beyond my eyes' reach, "Welcome back. Do you feel okay?"

Unable to define 'okay', my mind struggled to answer. Still trying to piece together this strange scene and the thousands of journeys I had just been on, a slight sound escaped my lips and it frightened me. Then I felt what had brought me here in the first place. Fear. Fear was cold steel. It was the prison bars built around my very flesh that had kept my soul inside. Fear had been one of my first life lessons and one I had learned repeatedly. Faithfully I clung to it as if it was the water that quenched my thirst, and yet it had parched me instead. The more I drank of fear, the more I sought out a remedy to help me escape the prison that fear had built around me.

My heart beat was electronic. It beeped next to me on a screen, and this elevated my prison. My existence was reduced to an electronic model on a machine next to my bed. My whole life was reduced to a screen. I wanted to dream again.

She moved closer, her voice like a blanket that briefly covered the cold steel. "My name is Grace, I'm your nurse for the next eight hours. You're going to be okay." She continued, "You've got to stop trying to kill yourself."

It was dark, but I could hear the smile in her voice. She was assuming it was an accident, like I just partied too hard and ended up here. She didn't understand my desperate need for flight. The average person didn't understand or care to know they were trapped. This mundane world quenched every desire they had, so they were comfortable in the roles they had been acting out in this Earthly scene. I, however, was bursting at the seams. My soul struggled for freedom, and yet the steel bars of fear pinned me inside. My soul screamed from thirst, and I fed it alcohol. Then, I fed it heroin. And when my soul awoke from its stupor, I fed it more. I spent half my life trying to stifle my own spirit.

"I'll check on you in a little while. Get some rest," she whispered, and the door clicked behind her.

I closed my eyes in prayer, folding my hands across my stomach. Lungs tight and body weak, I prayed silently, "God, show me a way out. Please, let me unlearn the fear of everything this world has taught me to be afraid of. Show me freedom from within."

I drifted off, and my soul began to fly again. I dreamt of places and events where I meant something to people, where I had purpose, and where I loved myself enough to let others love me. I dreamt the unimaginable; I was no longer stuck within the confines of my own needs, desires, and fears, but I lived for something greater. I had impact and purpose. I could change the course of not only my life, but this entire reality. I could influence others, and then this world. I dreamt I was just as capable as each and every one of you…that I was a creator.

Little did I know, all dreams can come true. Years later I would finally begin to manifest them.

FALLING

*"The Sun comes up and goes back down,
Falling feels like flying til you hit the ground."*

—Chris Stapleton

I'VE HAD DREAMS throughout my life that I was falling. Eventually, I discovered this isn't an anomaly and is actually quite common among other people. Even more common for me are the dreams I often have of jumping. I begin by jumping over small obstacles, and then larger things like trees and houses. And in the dream, I'm thrilled at this new physical gift of mine. Ultimately though, in every single dream like this, I end up leaping miles into the sky until I'm past the point of no return. The journey up is exciting and exhilarating, but at some point I realize the situation I've put myself into and as my jump slows to a halt, I reverse directions in mid-sky. That's when terror sinks in, the descent. On the way down my body is immersed in extreme fear. Ironically, I am often lucid enough in the dream to think, *I hope this is only a dream again and not real.* And as usual, mid-fall my eyes crack open before I hit the ground. I'm awake. My pulse returns to normal, and I lie there wrapped in a warm blanket, clutching my pillow, relieved to see sunshine peeking through the draperies.

When I was only a child, another child told me that if we hit the ground in a dream, then we die in reality. What a scary thing to hear! I prayed I never fell again. I still did, many times, but I never crashed to the ground. I believed this myth for many years; certain it must be true. It was strange once I realized that others have these same dreams, and even more odd that no one dreams they hit the ground.

Addicts and alcoholics tend to sugarcoat our own self-destruction in order to make it more palatable for ourselves, as well as tempt others to swallow our lies and sit in our pit of misery with us. A certain level of this self-destruction, we call 'getting high', is nothing remotely like what drugs do to us. In fact, quite the opposite. Instead of lifting us up to higher levels, drugs bring us down to low, basic levels of existence. The reality is drugs and alcohol slow our spirits, to make room for our lowly, carnal nature. Here, we care about nothing but sex, food, sleep, and comfort at whatever risk. The term 'getting high' may have initially described the more non-addictive drugs like marijuana, LSD, mushrooms, peyote, etc. These drugs have been used to access various mental levels of consciousness and have even been used in psychological research, mental health treatments, and spiritual ceremonies for transcendence. So, the term 'getting high' applied to drugs such as cocaine, opiates, benzodiazepines, meth, and alcohol couldn't be more of a deception. These drugs take away all higher perception and abandon us in immediate ego-based existence. Under the influence of these drugs, we exclusively seek our own self-satisfaction.

On a large scale these drugs pull us to lower levels of existence by taking over our lives and holding our hearts and minds hostage through addiction. We live in an ego-controlled world where nothing matters except our self-fulfillment. All higher levels of emotional, mental, and spiritual consciousness only come and go in vague waves that seem like distant memories or brief flashes of guilt and remorse across the new smokescreen of our mind. Yet, we call this getting high.

It's easier to ingest when we ignore the fact that we are falling; when we convince ourselves we are flying. I saw a shirt once that said, "Drugs told me I could fly then took my wings." In active addiction, and I use that term interchangeably here with alcoholism, we are deceived into thinking we live in some secret world above everyone else. We are soaring above the clouds, worlds above the normal people below. We're soaring, but we have no wings. In early addiction we have yet to even break through the clouds and see that we are actually free-falling straight toward the earth.

Eventually we break through the clouds, and the awareness of our descent is inevitable. We can ignore it no longer. Some remain in denial until they inevitably crash into the ground and stay there, six cold feet below the surface. Most of us, however, fight the fall. We sense we are falling and in response, we instinctively flail against the sky, trying pointlessly to climb back up the air toward the point where our descent began. Our frivolous efforts bring about the same results as those who deny the fall. We never return to the heights. That is the deception of addiction. We never return to the 'good times' where it all began, when we were using and drinking just for fun, before those habits had fully destroyed our lives.

Once we realize we're not actually high, we're not flying, rather that we're falling, it's natural to fight the fall. Some fight it longer than others. It's exhausting and frustrating to wrestle the inevitable and make absolutely no progress. We lose hope, we lose faith in ourselves, we become disheartened, and we lose our will to fight anymore.

The fall is a nightmare. It is an endless cycle of pain, misery, and guilt. It is terrifying to know we are falling and realize nothing we do even slows our descent. All of our efforts are of no avail. The only thing we can do to end our plight is surrender to the fall. By the time this happens—if it happens—we've learned the hard way and have exhausted every other option. We must surrender to the fact that we cannot control this fall. We must cry out for help, reaching out to something outside of ourself, willing to surrender ourself and our will. We've learned repeatedly through failed efforts and mistakes that if we are to be saved from this fall, it must come from outside help. We surrender our fight, and then we must wake up. We shift our perception and awaken. It's not an immediate 'aha-moment', rather more of a very slow opening of the eyes. A small series of shifts in our consciousness lead us from one realization to the next until our eyes have fully opened to a new way of living.

First, we realize we were falling and not flying. We surrender our control. We reach out for help. We began to shift our perception from victimhood to personal responsibility. We let go of our ego, and we become open to learn and receive suggestions. All of these things can be found in the twelve-step programs, which some say are divinely inspired. Many have fallen before us, and many have awoken from their nightmare. They have indeed lit the path with inspiring words and actions we can learn from so that we may never fall again. Once we successfully awaken to a new way of living, it becomes our duty to then be a safety net to those after us who have finally surrendered to the fall.

I believe being able to clearly remember a dream offers a clue to something much deeper, especially a recurring dream that has come and gone throughout the course of one's life. Dreams are a portal to the subconscious, opening up a pathway between spirit and soul. Dreams speak to us in the same language Jesus spoke in, through the symbolic language of parable. It is a language that predates all written and oral language. It is the language of this planet and this universe in which nature is the dial plate of spirit, and the material world is but a reflection of the spiritual. As above, so below.

I was a jumper. I jumped over small things. I took risks. I dabbled in drugs and darker things, and I relished my willingness to go against the grain. I thought it made me important and special. I jumped higher. I went to extremes. Whatever any of my peers did, I always took it to the next level. I jumped so high into alcohol and drugs that I lost sight of the ground. I lost sight of any kind of normalcy, and I didn't care. I reveled in it. I was flying. I was way above everyone else, soaring, wings out, mocking those below me. Everyone could see I was falling, but me.

One day I looked to my left, I looked to my right, and I finally saw that there were no wings. I had been deceived the whole time. I was alone, and I was free falling through the cold layers of the atmosphere heading towards an inevitable death. I fought against the cold air for years until I was so exhausted that I let the fall cradle me instead. I had no choice but to fall. I reached out for help, I cried out, I screamed out for God to save me. When grace came, it wasn't in the way I expected. It came in the form of jails, and institutions, and hard life lessons. Still, I began to shift my perception and open my eyes. It's a miracle I didn't hit the ground. I woke up just in time.

I woke up into a new way of life, and I jumped in with both feet. I fell many, many times in the process as I tried to find the right way to fly. I tried many things to replace the wings I thought the drugs had given me. But no sooner had I taken off from the ground than I came falling back down. Thankfully, I hadn't gotten high enough to die from the fall.

Life is a never-ending series of lessons and growth. I've formed real wings now, real spiritual wings. I'm soaring now, but not looking down on anyone. I'm not alone either. There are millions of us, and much like a formation of geese flying through the air, we provide support and guide others alongside of us. If ever I try to replace these new spiritual wings with drugs, alcohol, ego or anything toxic, I will surely start the fall all over again. This I know I can count on as surely as the sunrise.

My only hope, if I ever fall again, is that I'm open enough to surrender and open my eyes before my body slams into the ground. Life is but a beautiful and tragic dream. In my previous book, *Chasing A Flawed Sun*, I walked the reader through my nightmare of falling. Now I present *Falling Towards Heaven*, my awakening from the nightmare and how I grew new wings.

Legend has it that Lucifer was once an angel until he fell. He fell from the most beautiful flight of all, soaring through heaven before he came crashing down to Earth, and never awoke during his fall. In all his bitterness and regret, he now obsesses over worldly things. Placing materialism over spirituality is inherently evil; it is the birthplace of all sin. Lucifer, the fallen angel, has become the king of all things sinful. He has been here since the beginning of humanity, deceiving us with greed, lust, and jealousy. He finds our weaknesses and exploits them.

Through his mastery of sorcery, he also became a drug dealer. The definition of magic and sorcery is to influence or sway reality using mysterious or unnatural forces. If I don't like the course of my life or my reality, I can alter it through magic. This is the traditional idea behind magic. In most cases magic has been thought of as creating formulas or potions using roots and herbs in order to derive certain results, empowering us to control our reality accordingly. Is this not what the pharmaceutical industry does? Is this not what drugs and alcohol when abused and used incorrectly do?

I used alcohol and drugs to either become someone who I didn't want to be, or to alter my reality into a much more tolerable state. Is this not sorcery? I tried to erase memories, or avoid obstacles. I tried to numb feelings, or build a false sense of self. This is the true meaning of sorcery. I tried to control my reality and my life through a chemical process, and as most selfish endeavors do, it backfired on me. There is only one pure way out, and that is the warrior's path. It is the slow way of building character and growing by facing life trials and tribulations head on and becoming stronger as you overcome each obstacle. There are no easy ways out. The valleys flood, and fake wings fail. As I've said a million times in my new life, the obstacles are the path.

The obstacles are always the path.

RUDE AWAKENINGS

DECEMBER, 1998

THE SOUND OF doors slamming in the distance and the quick-beep of horns signaling cars being unlocked woke me from my light sleep. The air inside the laundry room was dry and dusty, yet the old blankets and towels I had piled together as a makeshift bed between a dryer and a wall smelled extremely musty. Wiping the sleep from my eyes, I immediately wanted to light up a cigarette. I couldn't smoke in here in the morning though, not while the residents of the building were up and on the move. The smell of smoke might alert someone to come look inside and find me down here where I don't belong. The sight of a homeless junkie squatting in their building could threaten their whole ecosystem and the fabric that holds their seemingly perfect little worlds together. Without question, the police would be called, and I would be scolded and forced to leave, carrying my tattered belongings out with me into the rain to start all over again.

I climbed onto a washer to look out the small recessed ground level window into the parking lot. It was pouring, again. For three days straight it had been raining incessantly. It was as if the atmosphere reflected my pain. At this point in my life sunshine felt more like an insult, than a blessing. I didn't have the privilege of staying in and hiding from the rain either. For one, I didn't belong here, and the residents may be coming down to use the laundry room throughout the day. I came here late in the evening and left early in the morning. Secondly, I had to get on the move. My body was already frail and weak, but the more I awoke, the more the sickness would inevitably set in. My body craved heroin like the normal person craves water, only worse. I could go much longer without water than I could without heroin before I'd completely lose my mind. My arms were a smattering of black and yellow bruises among trails of red dots where dull needles had entered repeatedly. I was 19 years old but looked like I was 40, and my body was the size of a malnourished preteen. My life was a never-ending series of disappointments that I could only blame on one person, myself.

I had no one left. My own family had gotten restraining orders against me in order to protect their possessions from my thievery and my younger siblings from my influence. My only friends were other addicts I got high with, and they all scattered and disappeared when the money ran dry. I was alone and had been for a long time. I knew nothing but loneliness and felt much more comfortable there than I did with other people anyway. After all, there was no one left to disappoint or hurt when I was alone. All I knew was pain, which was occasionally interrupted by the soft bliss of a heroin high. The longer I used though, the shorter the highs lasted. I was feeling last night's high recede at that particular moment.

I knew that for every minute I was awake, panic, anxiety, and hyperawareness would come flooding in and intensify. Those feelings would soon be followed and intermixed with sickness. I had to force myself to get up and move, or I'd end up stuck in this laundry room physically and mentally tortured by the withdrawals. I had slept in my clothes. I always did. Thermal shirt, hoodie and baggy sweatpants hung from my skinny body. I also had a book bag full of stolen hygiene products that I scooped up and strapped over my shoulders. It was all I owned, and I knew it was going to get drenched by the rain. I had no choice but to walk out into it and get soaked. I had to move, and keep moving, until I found enough money to get well. 'Getting well' meant feeling normal again. I would shoot heroin just so I could function at a normal level. If I was lucky, it would be potent enough to give me a slight high. Once I had secured a feeling of normalcy, I could do regular things like eat a meal, and then return to my humble confines to go to sleep. Then I'd wake up and do it all over again.

I listened carefully until it was quiet in the building, slid out the door of the laundry room and up the stairs to the front door of the apartment building. Pulling my hoodie up over my head, I exited the front door into the rainy streets. The mall was about a half of a mile from there, and it was my only safe haven from the rain. I walked through the downpour as the rain drops pelted angrily at my hoody, and my sweatpants grew heavy from saturation. I was a madman, doing his daily walk of depression through the streets of a wet hell. My only reprieve was the shelter and opportunity of the local mall. There would be bathrooms for me to clean up in, dryness, warmth, and most of all, plenty of places to steal from.

When I arrived at the mall, I was an outsider. I was an alien visiting a foreign world. Among the hundreds of Christmas shoppers I stood out in my entirely drenched sweat clothes, still no one seemed to notice me. They buzzed around me in different directions weighted down with shopping bags, laughing and smiling, and carrying their coffees. I couldn't remember the last time I felt joy in the small things, or even the last time I openly laughed at anything. Life wasn't fun or funny anymore. It was a daily race for sanity and survival.

I headed straight for the bathroom to wash up, brush my teeth, and apply deodorant. Then I went outside of the mall to find a place to hide my book bag until later. I had to find a way to get money so I could get high, nothing could stop me on this mission. Outside of the mall, I knew where there were some bushes beneath an overhang, away from the rain's reach. I stuffed my book bag behind them and headed back inside.

The sound of Christmas carols played softly over the speakers in the hallways as I slinked my way through. I was an invisible ghost weaving through the crowds. The smells of candles and lotions coming from the various shops plagued my senses with holiday memories, and I was taken back. I stopped mid-motion and surveyed my surroundings. My wet clothes still clung to my frail body. People simply moved around me, some serious, some smiling, all of them dry and there to shop, not to steal like I was. "Jingle Bell Rock" played over the sound system while the scent of gingerbread lattes and pine scented candles took my mind down memory lane. I drifted back to Christmas at my parents' house, remembering how it was decorated every year the day after Thanksgiving. I smelled my mother's freshly baked cookies and saw the adorned tree in my mind's eye. As a child I could hardly sleep for weeks leading up to Christmas; it was the most magical season. Church on Christmas Eve meant singing "Silent Night" while holding candles in the dark, which always transported my mind and heart to far away Christmas lands. The holidays warmed my soul every year. Our family came together frequently with a grand finale on Christmas morning when we'd come racing down the stairs to a treasure trove of goods left by Santa himself.

Drifting back from idyllic memories, I found myself wet, standing in the middle of the mall again, focusing on the people around me. The music, the aromas, the smiles all reeked of holiday cheer. I was the grinch, a lecherous plague to the very environment in which I was standing. I was sick and ready to rob and steal whatever I could to get well. I was a disease to the Christmas spirit, a walking zombie, and an antithesis to everything this holiday stood for. There was no love, no cheer, and no joy in my life. I embodied pain, hurt, misery, and selfishness. The monster inside demanded to be fed. Despite the holiday joy I could smell and see and feel all around me, I still couldn't stop myself. The monster was hungry.

It took me less than an hour to work my magic. Even though I stuck out, I was seemingly invisible. I was easily lost in the crowds, and the stores employees were too busy to notice me stealing while everyone else shopped. I got what I needed and got out as quickly as possible. I was almost sad that I had to leave that magical Christmas wonderland and step back out into the rain to head to the bus stop. Soon I would be in a whole different world, one that reminded me of my future much more than my past. I'd head first to a pawn shop to trade these goods for money, then into the drug-infested neighborhoods of West Baltimore to get my medication.

The mall was a blessing and a curse. It provided me what I needed to get my fix, but it also reminded me of who I could've been and where I came from. It openly displayed the warmth of the lifestyle I chose to abandon through a series of poor choices. Now I had lost all control and was surviving only to feed a sickness that controlled me. I was injecting to live and living to inject. I was an invisible nothing with no purpose and no future.

I trudged to the bus stop, climbed onto the city bus heading downtown, and leaned my head against the window. Looking forward, I noticed a small wreath with a red bow hanging from the rearview mirror. It was staring back at me as the bus rattled and bumped through stop after stop on its way downtown. My head bounced against the window, and I let it in order to distract me from the sickness welling up within. The wreath seemed to stare back at me, at the pathetic lump of me. It peered into my soul, my pockets full of stolen goods, my heart as cold as ice. The ride seemingly took forever. I had to get away from that wreath, from that mall, and into the thick of the streets. I had to get away from all the 'could've beens' and 'should've beens' and into the now. I had a demon to dissolve.

When the bus let off, I headed to the pawn shop. Then with new money in hand, I made my way to the dope strip. My body and clothes were soaked through again, but my money would stay dry. Balled up, and crumpled tightly in the palm of my hand, I wouldn't let it go until I had my sweet savior in hand. I walked through the rain even faster now. By the time I reached my destination, it had slowed to a soft mist, as if it was clearing a path towards my freedom. Eager to get well, I almost ran the last two blocks towards the drug spot. I rounded the corner breathing deeply, ready to buy two pills of scramble heroin from my usual guys. As I popped around the corner, a group of young guys standing against a brick wall turned immediately in my direction.

Before I could say anything, one of them yelled out, "Ayo, let me get five dollars, boy."

I ignored him and asked the others, "Who's out? Is B out?" I was focused on getting my heroin.

"Fuck I just say? Lemme get five dollars," he barked.

"Nobody's out today?" I asked, desperately now, wondering why the block was empty except for these guys.

"Come here, junkie, I got something," one of them said.

I could tell something wasn't right. I could feel their energy, and they were up to no good. I quickly turned to walk away.

"Don't ignore me. Come here, boy!" one shouted behind me. Then I heard their footsteps. They were loud in my ears like a small stampede catching up to me. I winced because I already knew what was coming. I felt a foot land in the middle of my back as I went spinning forward into the street. I slid across the wet ground as another foot connected squarely in my face.

"Fuckin junkie, yo!" one of them said before he spit on me as my nose opened up, gushing blood onto my lips.

I scrambled to my feet, slipping and skidding across the wet pavement, barely dodging another blow as they came after me. I clutched my cash for dear life as I ran. I made it off the side street and onto a busier street as horns blew at me while I dodged through traffic bringing one car to a screeching halt. The boys had already stopped chase and turned to walk back up the block. I bowled over breathing heavily, tasting blood, as I watched them walk slowly up the street. I was like a sick, weak gazelle who had just barely escaped a pack of hyenas. Now I was even more broken than before.

I wanted to give up. But like so many times before when I wanted to give up, the unrelenting sickness and terror took over. Those feelings were worse than any beating or any physical pain, so giving up was never an option. I stumbled into a McDonald's, and the patrons looked at me in disgust. Still soaked from the rain, I now had blood running down my face.

I was white and frail, so it wasn't hard for onlookers to figure out what I was and what I was doing in this part of town.

I stumbled into the bathroom, aching and ashamed. Even in this pit of despair I hadn't lost my ability to be embarrassed of what I had become. I was beyond repair and couldn't begin to see a way out. I headed to the sink and began to rinse my face with cold water, wiping away the blood with paper towels. I would have cried, but my tear ducts dried up a long time ago. Worse than any of the physical pain I felt was the impending sickness, and I still had the money to get rid of it. I had to get back into the streets and quickly.

After wiping my face clean, I walked out of the McDonald's and refocused on the mission ahead of me. There were hundreds of other places to score heroin in the city, I would just have to hop back on the bus and get away from this area today. As I walked back towards the bus stop, I happened to look across the street where my beating had just taken place. My guy "B" was standing on the side of the busy street waving in my direction. My heart raced; I was going to get well. I moved quickly across the street to my savior for today, eager to hear what he had to say. As I approached him, he gave me a look of mock concern.

"Yo, how much you got?"

"Twenty," I replied, and before I could tell him what just happened, he cut me off.

"I heard what them boys did to you. I handled that. Don't worry about that shit again. Your money's always good here."

I handed him my twenty dollar bill, and he reached into his pocket and handed me something back. It didn't feel like pills of dope. He noticed the confusion on my face and cut me off again.

"It's something new. Trust me, you'll love it." And with that he walked back up the block.

I quickly opened up my hand to examine the sealed wax bag full of white powder. My heart bounced for a split second when I read the words stamped in red next to a small red musical note: 'Jingle Bell Rock'.

I floated through traffic, across the wet asphalt, and back towards the McDonald's down the street. I walked inside past the patrons dining there. This time I was neither embarrassed nor in pain because this time I had my medicine in hand and was ready to relieve myself of my inner plague. I knew when I walked back out, I would be a normal man again. I couldn't wait.

I walked into the empty bathroom, settled down in the stall, and pulled out my works. I dipped my needle into the toilet bowl after giving it one quick flush and pulled up some water. With trembling hands, I then cooked and drew up the mixture into my dull, worn out syringe. I stabbed my bloody arms three times before I was able to find a usable vein, but once I did, the rain stopped.

After four full days, the rain stopped. In fact, everything stopped, and I floated. My body slumped backwards and slid lifelessly onto the floor of that pissy McDonald's bathroom, and I drifted out of it. I drifted back into my mother's kitchen. Wrapped in the aromas of chocolate chip cookies and cinnamon sticks, my spirit danced. It soared through hundreds of candles that lined the darkness, sandwiched between the stained-glass windows of the church I once sang in on those magical Christmas Eves. It flew far away from the laundry room I had called home this week, far beyond the streets of West Baltimore. It was finally free.

I was finally uncuffed from the curse that ate away at my soul, from the eternal nightmare I trudged through day in and day out. There was no more pain and misery, and most of all, no one else to disappoint. Now I could start over, I could be who I wanted to be. I was free. A tear rolled down my lifeless body as I slumped on the floor against the cold toilet, my feet jutting out beneath the stall door.

I no longer felt the wet clothes that hung on my weak limbs. There would be no more stealing and lying, no more beatings and sickness, and no more worrying for my family. I was finally in a safe place. I was free and was returning home. The journey finally ended here in this bathroom stall, and I couldn't be happier. I no longer had to go to bed terrified and wake up terrified because of the impending sickness and feelings of depression and anxiety. I no longer had to live with or compile more guilt. I was afloat in space, returning home to the warm comfort of God. I floated blissfully, finally at peace, smiling because it was all finally over. I floated and floated dreamily until I was woken by an intrusive voice.

"We got him! He's alive!" a man exclaimed loudly.

My eyes snapped open and my body lurched forward. I was immediately launched back into existence and overcome with sheer terror. *Who is this? Where am I? Why would they do this?* My mind was racing. I tried to float, but I was up and heaving. *Why can't I get back to my floating?* My heart was palpitating.

"Sir, are you okay? Are you okay?" I heard a loud voice, and it reverberated through my body.

I ignored the question. I didn't want to speak. I didn't want to be here. I wanted to float.

"Sir, what is your name? Are you okay? You were dead. We just saved your life!" The horrible voice said.

I tried to hide from it. I needed to get away. My body was wrenching and shaking. I was deep in the stages of withdrawal. I could see the Naltrexone shot the stranger had given me laying on the floor next to me.

"Can you speak? Let me try to help you up," the voice said again. He had leaned down inches from my face, talking to me. Behind him I could make out a handful of McDonald's employees looking down at me with both interest and horror.

"Yes, yes, I'm okay," I muttered.

He extended his hand to me and grabbed mine, pulling me to my feet. I stumbled back into the wall for a second before gaining my balance. My body was on fire, my heart raced, and my anxiety came over me in waves.

"Why? Why would you do that?" I asked, terrified.

"Do what? Buddy, I just saved your life. You were gone! You should be happy!" He exclaimed.

He had no idea. I was happy, and he just stole that happiness from me. All I wanted to do was float. I had to get away from here. I had to run far away. This McDonald's bathroom was too bright; the voices were too loud. My mind was racing as fast as my heart. I was terrified.

"I've got to go," I said quickly as I moved past him for the door.

"Wait! The police are on their way!" He tried to grab my shoulder, but I shook him off as I marched out the door.

I walked out of the restaurant and into the cold, back into the rain. I walked as fast as I could into the city side streets. I didn't care if those young boys were out; they could beat me again. I didn't want to see that laundry room again. I didn't want to be anywhere except where I just got pulled back from. I just wanted to be floating, floating back through those magical Christmas memories growing up and floating back towards my creator. I wasn't that lucky though. Apparently, I didn't deserve any of that, I was meant to suffer.

I walked fast and hard, deep into the darkness of the city night. I had to find money. I had a sickness to get rid of. I had a monster to feed, and he was always hungry.

SQUARE ONE

Life is a journey,
and if you fall in love with the journey,
you will be in love forever.

—Peter Hagerty

I EMERGED FROM the pressure chamber with snow falling all around me. It was a new world out there, not because of any change in physical reality, but because of a slow shift in my perception. Intense pressure forms, molds, and ultimately creates the most valuable things in this world. For once, I felt like one of them. I had been in the final cooling off stages of my intense pressurization, the hardest parts months behind me now. The cooling off stage had transpired in my last and final drug rehab stay. As I walked away from it and into freedom, I kicked the snow out in front of me, and millions of little diamonds fluttered through the air. A world of possibilities lay before me, and for once I wasn't terrified.

I had always awaited my release from jails, prisons, and drug rehabs with both intense excitement and trepidation. I simply could never trust myself in the face of temptation. I couldn't trust myself to avoid self-destruction, subsequently hurting myself and everyone I loved. I was out of control, and my constant insistence that I could control my life drove me to the brink of insanity. My anxiety would skyrocket on the dates of my release, and with the first kiss of fresh air on my body came a sense of heightened awareness. My hyper-awareness came in sounds, light waves, smells, and colors. My nerves would push me into a panic, and I struggled to hold it inside so I wouldn't worry the family member who picked me up. They would make small talk, but my mind raced in all directions. They talked about where to stop for food, while my skin crawled. And when they inevitably began talking about the future and anything regarding a sense of responsibility, my heart would skip a beat sending shockwaves of pure panic coursing through my limbs. It was the same familiar result every time: I wondered how long it would be until I could get alone and find a way to make all of these horrible feelings go away.

This time was different. This time I didn't feel the same level of fear, though I thought I should. This time I felt wrapped in warmth, like an invisible security blanket as I trudged through the snow. I walked past liquor stores and bus stops. I had the freedom to go to all the familiar places, but I kept going forward without stopping. This time my perception had finally reached a new level where self-destruction wasn't my first response to freedom. This time, I did the right thing, and then the right thing again, and I basked in the temporary high of accomplishment that doing the right thing brings to someone who has never sought to do so. I was proud, and I lay down that night and a few following nights with growing confidence in myself and relief that maybe, just maybe, I could do this after all.

That's when I realized I had a hole to fill…

During my years of active addiction, all emotional and spiritual advancement ceased. I continued to grow physically and mentally. I aged physically under the influence of drugs and alcohol. Mentally, I still had the ability to grow and learn, to understand and embrace or reject changes in society, technology, politics, etc. However, drugs and alcohol brought my emotional and spiritual growth to a stifling halt. At no point during my days of using did I call on my Creator for anything except to pray for myself to benefit from some unfortunate situation I had landed myself into, including freeing me from the shackles of addiction itself. I was uninterested in forming a deeper connection to the Creator unless it benefited me. I wasn't looking to serve Him or anyone else above my own personal desires. My God served no other purpose in my mind than an empty sounding board at which I begged for leniency, then got frustrated when my pleas were not immediately answered. I did not deserve leniency, even though I was eventually granted it.

Emotionally, I was a baby. I started running from myself at such an early age that I hardly had any idea of who I even was yet. My alcohol use began at the onset of my teenage years and held me on a treadmill of emotional stagnancy until the drugs took over. The drugs numbed every single part of me, and the pursuit to find them during my sober hours consumed my every thought and action. Therefore, when I finally emerged from my substance-laced cocoon at age 23, I had the emotional capacity of a 12-year-old and was just beginning the early phases of spiritual growth.

Removing drugs and alcohol from my life after living an existence centered around them for so long, I discovered an obvious void inside. The void will consume anything in order to be filled, and still it is never completely satisfied. This, like everything else, I learned the hard way.

At completing my final court ordered treatment, I had secured a job at a local Pizza Hut as a waiter. With a criminal record containing multiple felonies, under court order, and on probation, there were very few jobs available to a young man like me. I never learned a skill growing up. My father was a real estate agent by trade, but I never spent much time around the family home. My addiction started so early that I never developed any hobbies that could generate enough skills for me to perform a trade, let alone play sports, or even learn how to socialize with people in a normal manner. The skills I had obtained like stealing, lying, selling drugs, fencing stolen goods, and figuring out ways around the rules would no longer serve a purpose on my new journey. I may as well have been 14 years old all over again filling out applications, nervous about whether I would fail and make a bumbling fool out of myself. Restaurants and warehouses had been my only options of employment throughout active addiction and would prove to be the only options granted to me in early recovery. Even those who were able to accept a record full of thefts and drugs like mine was were few and far between.

I was six months clean when I trudged out of that treatment center and had already been employed for three of those months through a work release phase. This was the longest period of time I had been clean outside of jail, and the first time I did not have even the slightest desire to return to alcohol. My parents let me come home for the first time in years, partially because I had no other options in place, but also because they had seen the changes in me. They had been down this road too many times in the past. They had listened to the promises and the talk of change only to be disappointed as I wandered into the house a day or two later nodding out over my dinner plate or stumbling in drunk at 4am. They would give me the usual ultimatum, watch me self-destruct for a couple days, and eventually put me back out into the streets. There comes a time when loved ones have no hope left and they lose faith in their addict, and rightfully so. There are only so many times a person can be bitten by a snake before they realize that it is, in fact, a snake. Some loved ones last longer than others. Some go deep into the stages of denial and codependence and become just as addicted and twice as affected as the addict himself.

I believe part of my parents' rationale for letting the snake back into their home was that they knew I would either end up serving a massive prison sentence or be found dead in the streets, and they likely concluded that these brief moments would potentially be the last ones we may ever share together. There are only so many times a person can receive broken promises before they become broken, and in turn so does the relationship. These relationships take many years to heal, and recovering addicts must remember that. I often thought I'd made a huge sacrifice to get clean and everyone should immediately respect that and adapt to it. I acted as if the world should bow down to my great accomplishment of sobriety. This is just more insane thinking. The only sacrifice I ever made was for the drug. I sacrificed my money and possessions, my loved ones, my pride and integrity, and ultimately my freedom for drugs and alcohol. By getting clean and remaining that way, I am simply doing what comes naturally to a normal, rational person. I do not deserve kudos for my own self-preservation.

I learned I must be patient and understanding with those around me, for my benefit as well as theirs. I had abused, lied to, and emotionally scarred the people in my life. I was a snake in their eyes, who could potentially strike at any moment, I learned that I had to be grateful for any second chance I was offered. There is an old joke that goes: "How do you know when an addict is lying? When their lips are moving." It's the truth. In active addiction I lied so much that I didn't even know when I was lying anymore. I lied to protect myself and those around me. I lied to myself, conned myself, and stole from myself. I lost sight of my emotions and my very soul, and in turn became almost sociopathic in my addict behavior, covering up my true identity in order to more fully pursue the chase. If I couldn't trust myself, how insane would it be to demand or expect trust from those I had hurt time and time again just because I had stopped using for a few days or weeks.

One example I'm positive a majority of addicts and alcoholics will identify with is the phone calls home from jail. I made dozens of them, and in my career as a bail bondsman I've listened to literally thousands of the same calls from men and women in jail calling home to talk to their parents, children, husbands, wives, etc. The phone calls are always full of promise and good news. The addict, once in jail with no access to drugs or alcohol is finally able to get in touch with their soul and emotions again, however painful it may be. This spills out over the phone as they promise the people they love that they are never going to drink or drug again, they are going to be a faithful husband or wife, they will go back to work and provide for their family, and that they will never do anything to come back to jail again. I can tell you from personal experience and through the hundreds of relationships I've forged with other addicts that they mean it. I'd venture to say 9 out of 10 of them mean it with all of their heart and firmly believe the words they speak over the jail phones. I meant every promise to stay clean and never return to jail. Every teary-eyed affirmation to be a good son, brother, or friend came from the heart. "This time will be different," I'd convince myself and those around me. Then within days, sometimes within hours, of release my promises were already broken.

I didn't even realize I was lying to myself because at the time I meant my words with every fiber of my being. Unfortunately, saying, "I'm never going to touch drugs again," is a lie if, in fact, I do touch drugs again. This in turn leads to an even worse conundrum. How do we survive in this world if we can't even trust ourselves? If the very words we speak from our hearts frequently become lies, how do we go on living a normal life after we realize this? When the one person we are stuck with and cannot escape is a liar and deceiver, the only way to shake loose of them is with alcohol or drugs, and so we keep using to maintain distance from ourselves at all costs. This is where surrender comes in, but I'll get to that later. The point is, as addicts, how can we expect our loved ones to trust us, when we cannot even begin to trust the words that leave our own mouths? The healing process does not happen overnight, therefore we must learn one of the most important attributes of recovery: patience.

I was completely unfamiliar with patience. My entire life to that point was spent tracking down everything I ever wanted it, the instant I wanted it. If it meant breaking the law or my own morality, well those were just the obstacles in the way of what I wanted. Now though in this new practice of recovery, I had vowed to myself to conduct myself with the very morals and integrity I had been raised with and had buried deep down inside all these years. This meant I had to learn patience because I could no longer force things to go my way, nor could I afford to give up and walk away. If employers wouldn't hire me, family members didn't trust me, and old (positive) friends were leery of me, then I had to accept that. I had to accept the fact that it was my fault. I was not the victim here; most of the time they were. A painstakingly slow shift in my perception moved me from self-absorption to understanding. If I wanted to stay clean, I could no longer play the role of a victim.

Naturally, working this out was much easier said than done. When I moved from the town where the rehab was located in the suburbs of Northwest Baltimore to my parents' house about an hour away, I also relocated to the Pizza Hut in that town. I no longer worked for the pretty young manager who secretly doubled as my female companion, and who adored me and understood my history. I was now under the authority of strict managers who had no inclination to coddle me or understand my history of drug abuse. At no point in my life had I ever been able to follow the directions of authority if I didn't agree with them. If the person in authority wasn't equipped with a gun, taser, and/or nightstick, I would more than likely either tell them to fuck themself or agree to their face and disobey behind their back. Even when the authority was equipped with the aforementioned tools of the trade, I still usually pressed on with my rebellion until my luck ran out.

When I transferred to the new location to wait tables, there was instant turmoil between me and the management. They insisted I shave the small thin line of a beard I had grown on my face since I was old enough to grow facial hair. I wasn't ready to accept that change, so I argued and ignored their requests until I was sent home one day. I disobeyed their smoking rules and snuck out whenever the urge hit me, and I was reprimanded repeatedly. Instead of following the rules, I became a victim in my own mind. The rules didn't make sense to me, so I concluded they shouldn't apply to me. I was still living in a self-centered prison, and as long as my world revolved around my wants and needs, then everyone who imposed their own wants and needs into my world was an oppressor. I dismissed the truth that the manager had a problem with me because I never followed rules, and instead determined in my mind that she didn't like me because she had a son who had passed away from heroin many years earlier. I felt horrible for her loss, I truly did. I tried to be friendly with her and appease her, but I still was not willing to leave my own comfortability in order to follow her rules. I was selfish. So, when I walked out to serve a drink to a table, and she demanded that I come back to the kitchen and put the drink on a tray rather than hold it in my hand, I quit. I took my apron off and threw it in the trash in front of her, and said, "Fuck this job," and a barrage of other insults as I stormed out the door. I was still sick, and I didn't even realize it.

Just like the many times in my youth when I would brag about the horrible things I had done to other people, I bragged about the way I quit that job and the many names I called her. I read people's faces as I relayed these stories and was internally confused as to why they weren't impressed. The world around me had matured and I had not. My behavior was far from what recovery was supposed to be.

I should have learned these principles in the meetings of Narcotics Anonymous and Alcoholics Anonymous, but I didn't. I went to meetings every single night for at least the first six months of recovery, and I must have listened just enough to hold onto a thread of hope. I was doing the bare minimum by showing up. One thing became more important to me than my own recovery, and kept me coming back to the meetings—and that was women. Women became my new obsession, and if I gave them enough power in my mind to stay just out of reach then they would keep me coming back day in and day out for the thrill of the chase. I often wonder if the meetings had not been not coed if I would have gotten clean. I'm not saying the meetings kept me clean, but they gave me a strong foundation from which to build from. They gave me structure in early recovery and something to do with my time. Outside of that, I was constantly looking to fill a hole within myself with the first thing I always ran to, and that was attention from the opposite sex.

I had all of the answers. Much like a teenager, there was nothing anyone could tell me. I didn't realize that emotionally, I still was a teenager. Remember, I was operating with a four-teen-year-old's heart when I entered the rooms of Narcotics Anonymous hoping to catch the attention of women who were just as sick as I was. I was obsessed, and my obsession blocked me from the insight that I can clearly look back with today. What did I have to offer anyone? I had lived my life as a drunk, drug addicted criminal with no career, no trade, and no experience. I was fresh out of jail and rehab, living in my parents' basement. My brain and emotions were a toxic swamp, and I was a spiritual baby just learning how to crawl and live life all over again, and I wanted to offer *that* to someone?

Water seeks its own level, so the only females I was going to attract were those fresh out of, or still in, halfway houses who were just as emotionally immature and torn apart as I was. Together we would equally destroy each other. I had the irrational thought in my mind that I would instantly attract a woman ahead of me in the game of life, one who would take care of me and show me the ropes. After all, I deserved that, my ego assured me. I spent the first half of my life with this dis-illusion about women and my own over inflated sense of self.

The women kept me coming back though. I put together my best outfits, and worked hard to afford brand name clothes and new sneakers. I came into the meetings dressed as fresh as I could and went everywhere else in life the same way, and I left frustrated that nobody would speak to me. I would sit in the rooms and daydream while the speakers talked, trying to make eye contact with any attractive women in the room. They rarely played the eye contact game back. It didn't matter how much I dressed up I was still me. I was still the shy, quiet, nervous 14-year-old I had been before I started drinking to make all those insecurities go away. I hated my sober self.

I spent enough time in those meetings to absorb some of the wisdom and lingo, and the techniques and skills addicts use to stay clean. I knew almost everything there was to know about recovery, however the work to apply it and the change it required was too much. Instead I sat in those rooms and reasoned in my ego fueled mind how no one was as tough as me, had been through what I'd been through, was as cool as me, or sold drugs like me, etc. These ego inflated notions quickly became the walls of insecurity I built around myself because deep inside I really believed I was worthless.

As a young person entering society, I built up walls and facades not just to protect myself, but to hide my weakness, fears, and insecurities. I carried out a tough image of myself and let my ego dictate my actions, pretending to be someone I really wasn't. It took heroin to strip down every wall I built, every false image I carried, and every mask I wore. Heroin stripped me bare and pushed me to find my natural self again or die. Yet here I was in recovery building up the same walls and an egotistical image of myself to protect myself from fear instead of addressing the root causes of my fear. If I wasn't careful, history would repeat itself, I would be doomed, and heroin would either break me down again or kill me.

I judged everyone around me, and so I struggled trying to make friends with them. I went out with groups for meals after the meetings, played cards at their houses, and hung out various places, but I always felt like the outsider in the crowd. Still, I continued to force these interactions on myself because I was told that was what I was supposed to do for recovery. I had nobody else. I certainly couldn't go back to hanging with my old friends because that meant certain death. In the beginning, that was one of the few things I actually got right.

After walking out on my job at Pizza Hut, I knew I had to find work immediately. I couldn't possibly afford all the fresh clothes to impress the women who I shouldn't be trying to impress since I didn't have a job. Not to mention, I was living under my parents' roof as a full grown adult, and they wouldn't allow it if I wasn't working. I submitted applications everywhere, did job fairs, went to the county social services job search office and learned how to actively operate their system to locate employers who were hiring. I put in hundreds of applications, mostly for jobs I wasn't experienced in. Still, the majority of them rejected me instantly because I had to check *yes* next to the box that inquired, "Have you ever been convicted of a felony?" I had learned this lesson the hard way once during my addiction.

Years prior, when I was leveled out on the methadone treatment around 1999, I was job searching and had applied at a bank near my home. To my surprise they called me in for an interview, and then I was even more surprised to be asked for a second interview. I had previous seasonal experience working as an accounting clerk for two different tax firms while I was on methadone and partially free from street drugs, which helped me get my foot in the door for the bank interviews. Frustrated that I had been denied job after job due to my criminal history, I decided to lie about it on the application. After my second interview I received a phone call advising me I was hired and that I'd have to attend training in the city of Annapolis for 40 hours, Monday through Friday the following week.

I attended the first day of training and did what I usually did in classrooms, I day dreamed and nodded out from the methadone. However, as the story of my life goes, when it came time to take quizzes and then the final exam, I would pass with flying colors. I was smart enough to be a danger to myself. On the first day of class I struck up conversation and began flirting with the prettiest girl in the class, who also turned out to be the regional manager's daughter. We discovered that we lived in the same county, and since it was an hour drive, we would carpool every day. This went well, and I was on the verge of forming a relationship and securing myself a solid spot in the company until the last day of class.

We both passed the final exam, and I was riding a high of accomplishment. We were on our way home and passing Baltimore City when I suggested she go into West Baltimore. I was going to score some heroin, and I suppose I thought I would impress her with my street savvy and knowledge of the hood. I'm not sure why, but she agreed. We pulled down on Edmondson Ave. and Brice St. deep in the heart of West Baltimore, and I scored some heroin. She said she didn't want any but didn't mind if I did it. I didn't have a habit because of the methadone, so I decided to hold it until I got home. We pulled up at the top of Edmondson and Fulton Avenues at a light, and two guys approached the car asking if we needed anything. I was driving her car because I knew the territory. When they approached the passenger side window, one of them reached in and snatched her purse off of her lap.

I knew I had just messed up big time. I threw the car in park in the middle of the intersection, uncertain how I was going to handle this. I was in a neighborhood with zero white people, and here I was in dress clothes from the training marching towards these two men as they sat on a brick wall rifling through her purse.

"Come on man, there's no fucking cash in there. You can't do anything with that shit. Let the lady have her purse." I was storming at them, looking like a frail twig in dress clothes. To my surprise one of them tossed it back, and I caught it as it flipped through the air.

"You're brave, I give you that. Now get the fuck out of here," he said.

And I listened.

She wasn't as impressed as I'd hoped because that was the last time I ever spoke to or saw her, until years later when she also had become a heroin addict.

I went to work in that bank branch as a teller. I counted money, handled money, and accessed the vault. After about a month I was randomly called into the manager's office and informed that I was being let go because my criminal background check had come back. I figured it already had and they had made an exception for me.

"I've already been working in the bank for a month. If I

had ill intentions, don't you think you'd have seen them by now?" I asked, pleading for my job. To no avail, I was fired. I walked out, angry at them and angry at the world, once again never taking personal responsibility. That was also the last time I ever lied about criminal history on a job application.

After a couple weeks of job searching, I gave up and went back to applying at restaurants for server positions. Still, I had a hard time finding employment. At this particular time in my life I was 23 years old and had held over 40 jobs. Some of them for only as long as two hours, some as long as nine months, but they were all on record as legitimate jobs. One of my job failures was a KFC where I worked coating chicken in batter. I was withdrawing from heroin and walked out after only two hours. Another was Ruby Tuesdays washing dishes. That lasted a couple of hours as well because I saw a tray of money in the empty manager's office and I helped myself to two twenties, dipped out the back door and caught a ride downtown. These employment stints were common in my history of active addiction, and yet here I sat with the nerve to be angry and frustrated that nobody was willing to hire me and give me a chance the moment I had gotten clean. Granted, these potential employers weren't aware of the things I had done. So finding it difficult to obtain gainful employment was karma. How could I be so self-centered to be angry that no one would hire me, when I hadn't proven myself to anyone and had burned every employer I had worked ever for?

I decided to try something new: an honest approach. I put in an application at a local Bertucci's Italian restaurant. I never heard back from anyone despite an ad in the local paper announcing they were hiring servers. Frustrated again, I called once, and then I made follow up calls every few days. I felt, for some reason, this was the right place for me. When I called I was very polite. Being polite was not hard for me, but making phone calls was. I was still shy, nervous, and introverted despite the tough exterior that I portrayed to everyone else. One day, I took a nosedive into my own anxiety and showed up at what I knew to be a slow time of day for the restaurant. I asked to speak to a manager. A middle-aged woman approached, looking busy and bothered, and I spilled the truth. I told her I needed a job, that I was an ex-addict and convict, that I had spent my life doing wrong. I explained that now I was on a new journey, that I would work any hours, and do whatever it took to be her best employee. The first 75 percent of my story sounded as if I was listing reasons for her not to hire me. What I had done here was surrender. I finally gave up. I stopped putting up a front. I stopped trying to control people and situations. Rather, I gave it all over to God and this woman in front of me, and I simply told the truth.

The woman's eyes broke with sweetness as she listened to my story. She responded, "Welcome aboard. I'm willing to give you a chance here. Don't make me regret it."

I didn't. I stayed with that company longer than she did, and when she moved on, I helped orchestrate her going away party. Almost twenty years later, and we still keep in touch to this day. I realize this isn't going to be everyone's results. After giving up, and pouring out my life story and all the horrible things that had brought me to that day, I was very prepared for her to shut the door in my face or blow me off. Maybe that is the result more often than not in these circumstances, however being honest is freeing. It is freeing to walk into a situation with sweet surrender, to have no secrets, so those who are there for you, both strangers and friends alike, can meet you on your level. Being honest with my potential employer gave us both freedom in the event anything happened in my life that was either a repercussion from my past or a backslide into it.

For a little while, I filled the hole addiction left with work. I worked as many shifts as I could. I picked up extra tables and charged other servers to do their part of the night side work. I came early and stayed late. It was something easy I could focus on, kind of like the simplicity of the heroin lifestyle. Instead of waking up and focusing all of my thoughts and emotion on chasing heroin, now I focused on my new hustle. As long as I focused on work, work, and more work, then I didn't have time to think about the anxiety-inducing aspects of real life; such as the fact I had no real plan for the future, that I was 23 and living in my parents' house, and the only real future I had was waiting tables. These were the kinds of things I thought about in my idle time, and in the early stages of recovery they were enough to drive an overactive brain like mine into anx- iety attacks and depression—and potentially either relapse or suicide. So I did what I knew best, I built a wall between myself and my thoughts with more work. The only problem was that all this work I was doing was only bringing in just enough money to spend on brand name clothes and shoes. Sometimes I managed to save up enough to buy a gold ring, bracelet, or chain. I had no bank account, and who cared if I didn't have money as long as I looked like a million bucks, right? I assumed the people around me couldn't see past my facade. I mean, if I had fooled myself into thinking I was the toughest, coolest, most attractive guy around, then everyone else was sure to believe it too.

In my idle time, I attended meetings and played cards with

the people in the meetings. I had a couple of random one-night stands with women in the program to temporarily fuel my ego, but no luck finding myself a girlfriend. Looking back, I think that was God sparing me from my own self-destruction and halting the growth that having a girlfriend at that time in my life would have brought on. Instead in my own sick mind I found other ways to fuel my ever-hungry ego. I found online chatrooms, and dating websites. Here I could chat up strange women regularly and eventually end up going to their houses and sleeping with them. These were usually not the most physically attractive women, however when seeking to feed a sick ego, none of that mattered. My conquests were based on ego more than lust because the majority of the time I wouldn't even reach orgasm, and sometimes I struggled to even get an erection. The more attractive I found a woman to be, the more nervous I became, and the more nervous I became, the more my nerves prevented me from enjoying the moment (and certain parts of my body from enjoying the moment as well). I have never been the type to be able to make love to a woman without at least having some kind of an emotional connection. I always envied the animalistic ability of other men to have sex with any women at the drop of a dime, and instantly have no problem maintaining an erection doing so. Again, because I had yet to emotionally and spiritually mature, I viewed an asset as a liability.

My ego was a monster, and now looking back at life and watching others go through the various ups and downs I have already been through, I can clearly see how the ego is a defense mechanism. The less we value ourselves, the more we feed our ego. Generally, those with no money, no integrity, and nothing to lose, walk around with their chest poked out and a chip on their shoulder. Those who don't value themselves cannot fathom how to value another human being, especially of the opposite sex. In my recovery, I didn't use women, I didn't lie to them about my intentions. If I was only after sex, then I made that very clear. However, I didn't value them either. If I valued them, I wouldn't have played upon their weaknesses, whether they agreed to it or not. I say this because almost every one of the women I slept with wanted something further, even after I made it clear what my intentions were, and I'd eventually have to excommunicate from them. Then like any self-consumed addict, I'd pop back up at times when I needed sex to fulfill either my lustful desires or those of my ego.

I hadn't left the gym either; I was still going regularly. I believe that the gym or any other fitness regimen is a huge benefit to one's recovery. However, like everything else in life, I became obsessed with it. As I began seeing physical changes in body, my ego swelled as well. I obsessed over building my body and getting a six-pack. The responses I received from women online only fueled my ego, although those I ran into in person showed no interest. I neglected to take in the fact that they were just as insecure and shy as me. The other more outgoing, predatory types of males generally hustled all the women in the meetings. In response I took up the attitude that I didn't want to date a woman in recovery anyway, that it was too dangerous to my sobriety. This was only partially true. Had an attractive woman in recovery approached me or given me enough signs she was interested, I would have thrown that excuse right into the garbage with every other protective statement I ever crafted to defend my pride.

I began lifting weights back when I was in prison. I was

always an extremely small guy from childhood on up, so any physical progress I made in the gym still left me being exceptionally small. However, in my mind, I belonged on the cover of Muscle & Fitness magazine. Once I had been home for a couple weeks and joined a gym, I began working out faithfully. I was able to buy protein and control my diet, and so I had gotten myself up to a whopping 165 pounds and thought I was huge. Like any typical egocentric male, I used shirtless pictures of myself with my abs showing to drum up attention on the internet, so I could continue to feed the monster within. Instead of getting turned on by the women I slept with, I would instead get turned on by their reaction to my appearance.

Life wasn't entirely full of games though. As much as I kept trying to stuff it down and stay in the moment, there was an inevitable future I would have to face. At that moment, I had none, and that was scary. My parents had grown weary of having an adult in the house who worked out all day, then waited tables and stayed up on the computer all night month after month. There clearly was no end in sight to my behavior and so I was given an ultimatum: move out or go to college.

At that point in time there was only one thing that made sense. My criminal history made it almost impossible for me to get a job in the majority of available fields. I had no real passion to pursue a career in any field that was willing to accept me, if there even were any. The only areas where I had experience was with the law and with drugs. Those were two things I knew inside and out. I would have loved to have been a police officer and worked my way up to detective. Solving puzzles and mysteries was right up my alley. Unfortunately, the police force was never known to hire criminals, or at least those who had been previously caught. There was only one choice, in my opinion, and that was to become an addiction counselor. It was the only thing that made sense. I had survived drug addiction, and now it was my turn to share my wealth of knowledge with those who had gone down the same path as me. Most of my previous counselors in the facilities I had been to were former addicts, and many of them claimed to have extensive criminal records similar to mine. Finally, I decided, I had a solid plan and mission in life.

I applied for student aid and government loans at the local community college, and I was approved rather quickly. Next, I registered for the upcoming semester. I would have to take about two years of general studies in the Harford Community College, and then another two years of field-related classes in the neighboring Baltimore County Community College. This, I knew would at least buy me four more years at my parents' house. I was honestly afraid of living anywhere else. I had spent half of my life already living outside of their home, but none of those times were spent sober. I had no idea how to live on my own and maintain my sobriety, and the thought terrified me. However, the thought of living out my years as an adult in my parents' house was just as frightening. When all of these thoughts created anxiety, I could either go to a meeting or jump online and get attention from a woman to take my mind off. More often than not, the latter won out.

I continued to hustle waiting tables fulltime. I was great at reading people's emotions, wants and needs, and taking care of them. In the front of the restaurant among my tables I was a very kind, pleasant, caring server with a soft, higher-pitched voice. In the back of the restaurant, I was a foul-mouthed gangster. This two-faced persona is something almost every waiter and waitress learns to perfect, and mine was a bit more extreme than most. I began to forget what a blessing my job was and take it for granted. I still had a bit of destructive nature in me. If someone told me I couldn't smoke, I would sneak out anyway. I practically lived in the smoke area out back. The restaurant had stucco walls on the exterior, and we quickly learned that silverware, when thrown, would stick into the wall. Within weeks there were hundreds of knives and forks stuck into the walls around the building high enough that no one could pull them out. I would take firewood and dishware and toss it up onto the roof in an attempt to humor those around me. Maybe, in my mind I was rationalizing that the company owed me for how much time and effort I dedicated to them over the years. Clearly, this was backwards, self-consumed thinking. They owed me nothing more than the money I earned, and they had given me the opportunity to do so.

Still I continued to be a prankster at work. I would hide crayons in the cheese graters beneath the parmesan cheese. When another server delivered entrees to their table and the diner asked for fresh grated cheese on their lobster risotto, the patron watched in horror as the server unknowingly grated blue crayon all over their dinner. The managers would explode in fury, and no one would fess up. I never shared my pranks with anyone. Those who knew wouldn't dare rat on me. I still thought violence and deviance was a solution to life's problems, a pleasant distraction.

I had started going out with all of the other waitstaff at the end of our shifts. They were avid drinkers and pot smokers and occasional cocaine users. I would usually hang with them for the early part of the night, either at a local TGIFridays or at a house party, before the drugs came out. These definitely weren't ideal situations to put myself in, but one thing I did right was to let everyone know exactly where I stood in my recovery and how serious and proud of it I was. This didn't keep everyone from forgetting, especially when they got drunk, not to bring me back a shot from the bar or offer me a drink. However, I had no problem telling them no. I was very proud of my recovery, and one thing I knew for sure was that I would not drink again under any circumstances. If they got too pushy, I threatened them with violence, as it was the only solution I had ever learned was effective from my old way of life.

I was lonely. I went to the gym by myself, I went to college by myself, and I worked. I didn't get off from most of my shifts until after 10 PM, so my meeting attendance fell by the wayside. I still went occasionally, but I had to choose between my job and meetings, and I felt like I needed the job more at that point. *If I feel myself slipping, I will go back to the damned meetings*, I would tell myself. *I've come far enough, I can function well now.* And I often rationalized to other people, "The meetings are my doctor, and if I feel like I need to see a doctor, then I will return." The problem was this: drugs and alcohol are only the symptom of a greater issue within. And that had to be addressed before real recovery was possible. As usual I did the bare minimum and neglected the hard part.

I was an exception to the common rule of thumb and stigma regarding addiction. I came from a two-parent home. I was never molested or suffered serious trauma as a child. Neither of my parents were addicts, nor had they ever touched a drug. According to the common stigma regarding addicts, one or all of these scenarios are required to complete the recipe of dysfunction that creates an addict and/or alcoholic. This is simply not true. I know many people just like me who come from the same, if not better, backgrounds than my own. My family was not wealthy by any means. In fact, my parents were bankrupt in my youth, but they managed to supply all my needs fully. I know many addicts who have come from wealth, and had no trauma or missing parents. I also know addicts whose mothers gave them their first shot of heroin, who were repeatedly raped and abused as children, who lost both parents, or watched family members die tragically. There is no set mold that defines who will or will not become an addict. There is no certain discipline, or parenting style, or even surroundings that will prevent addiction, although certain factors may decrease the risk. If we could pinpoint the specific criteria that create addicts, we would be no closer to a solution because it would vary according to every addict we encounter. More so, I believe addiction is a process. Just like getting clean is a process, and recovery is a process, I believe becoming an addict or alcoholic is also a process that happens over a period of time up until the first drug or drink is consumed, and then it is confirmed.

There was something wrong with each and every addict. A hole that was created, or we were running from something, and drugs and alcohol filled that hole and/or helped us hide. We can remove the drugs and alcohol, but without really addressing the root issue that led us to abuse drugs and alcohol in the first place, we are never going to truly live our most fulfilling life. Instead, we are just ticking our days away, white knuckling it through an almost meaningless existence. I want everyone to recover. This is why the twelve steps of Alcoholics & Narcotics Anonymous were created. It's what most religious and spiritual paths were created for. We must look deep within and get to know ourselves, before we can begin to understand and address the issues that led to our self-destruction. Believe it or not, as commonplace as it seems, self-destruction is not normal.

At this point, I had addressed absolutely nothing within myself. I had no clue who I was or why I did what I did, and yet here I was going to school for chemical dependency counseling. I dove into life and took back control of my surrender. I lost my humility, and gratitude, and almost lost everything.

The college classes were a waste of time and money because ultimately they only snowballed into a massive amount of debt that years later Sallie Mae came looking for, and I had never completed what I set out to do. I was still of the mindset that "I want what I want, and I want it now!" This is typical addict mentality and the way I and people like me had become accustomed to living. Something like college was exciting for the first month or two, but the fact that I wasn't receiving any immediate benefit from it meant that it was no longer a priority in my life. So college went where everything else that didn't bring me immediate satisfaction went: on the back burner, along with the meetings and my spiritual relationship with God.

There was a female named Maria at work. I was drawn to her and we spent time together outside of work. We were very similar, with the exception that she had never been an addict. Within a couple nights, we slept together. I intended to make this one of my usual one-time things. However, one time turned into two times, which turned into many times. Most nights, we both finished work when the rest of the world was going to sleep, so as much as I tried not to get into any semblance of a relationship with her, it began to happen. I was not ready to settle down. I had chased heroin for my prime teenage years and early twenties without ever caring about sex or women. Now, I was making up for lost time. I couldn't bear the thought of giving myself entirely to one woman and missing more of my prime years of fun unless I was head over heels in love. I didn't know what love was, I thought I had felt it strongly at one time, but looking back I was positive it was the drugs. With this girl, I told myself I would keep a distance, and yet here I was at work with her every day, and then outside of work with her at night. I tried to push her away, be mean, give her attitude, but that wasn't easy for me because it wasn't who I was. I'd eventually apologize, only to repeat the cycle. I appreciated her and the fact that she really liked me. I believe that in the beginning I only loved her because she loved me. She truly, completely cared about me at a time when, unbeknownst to me, I still wasn't ready to love myself.

Six months in, I committed to a relationship with her, but never stopped fueling my ego with other women. I still occasionally would sleep with another woman if the opportunity presented itself. I was nowhere near ready to be in a relationship because I was not even capable of loving myself yet. If I truly loved and accepted myself, I wouldn't have to seek validation from other women to continually have my ego stroked. The majority of the women I slept with were women who were less attractive than my girlfriend, and some of them I wouldn't be seen in public with. This of course speaks more to my own defects of character at that time. I cheated throughout the course of that relationship and sometimes spoke openly about it. I would even make comments in front of her to insinuate what I was doing in order to prepare her for the eventual revelation of my bad deeds. I would make selfish comments like, "You know I didn't want to be in a relationship in the first place," or "I'm not relationship material." The damage I imposed on her was because I was still broken inside, and yet I believed and acted as if I had it all together.

I carried on for about another year this way until my recovery was tested and all the walls I had built came crumbling down around me.

LEVEL TWO

I climbed a mountain and I turned around
And I saw my reflection in the snow-covered hills
'Til the landslide brought me down

—Stevie Nicks

I'M NOT SURE why they are called wisdom teeth, but in the end they made me a little wiser. The pain in my mouth had become excruciatingly strong, and it prompted me to see a dentist, and then an oral surgeon. I was about three years clean and a nervous wreck when I was told I'd need dental surgery. I wasn't worried about the surgery itself; I was worried about how I was going to recover without taking painkillers. All four teeth needed to be removed at once, according to the expert in front of me. That was the quickest and easiest way to do it.

"Okay, but I have to let you know that I'm a recovering addict and alcoholic," I stated proudly.

"That's no problem, I've worked with your kind before. Just remind me on the day of surgery," he responded flatly, without the accolades for my sobriety that I secretly craved. I felt like I was being brushed off and not taken seriously.

A couple of weeks went by, and as we got close to the appointment my anxiety was on high. I had been with Maria for about a year at this point, and she knew how serious it was to me as a recovering addict to avoid the painkillers or anything that would threaten my sobriety. She also knew I wouldn't be able to drive immediately after the procedure, so she volunteered to go with me for support and to drive me home. Once I was called into the operating room, I invited her to come with me. I was grateful for her support and felt like I needed her there with me. As the oral surgeon explained the full procedure to us, and the recovery process, I interrupted him to remind him of my history of drug addiction.

"Well, typically we prescribe a couple weeks' worth of painkillers, like Percocet, to be used as needed. You are definitely going to need something, I promise you," he said.

"Absolutely not. I can't," I replied.

He shook his head and chuckled to himself.

Maria interjected, "He's serious. I don't think you understand."

To which the doctor replied, "I don't think you understand. This is a very painful procedure and recovery. His teeth are impacted. You cannot simply go without pain medication after something like this."

We went back and forth, as he declined to take me seriously. Finally we came to an agreement.

"Three days!" I said. "Give me three days worth of medication, and that's it. I can handle that."

After that conversation the last thing I remember was being injected with valium. I remember clear as day, as I awoke in a drug induced stupor, Maria was standing beside me and smiling down at me trying to hide her concern. I was still reclined, practically flat in the dentist chair.

I looked up at her and said, "Can you please take me downtown? I need to go downtown." Then I don't remember much else, including the car ride home. Going downtown meant going to Baltimore to cop heroin. She knew enough to know what I wanted. When I was coherent enough to hold a full conversation with her, I was shocked at the recollection my own words. A few years without a single drug or drop of alcohol, and all it had taken was a shot of valium, and my first thought upon waking was to score some heroin. Drugs and the grip that they can have on the human psyche is both fascinating and terrifying.

Before heading home we stopped at the pharmacy. The doctor's feeble attempt to acknowledge my addiction was to prescribe the lesser of two evils: Oxycodone instead of Percocet. Still, he wrote the prescription for fourteen days. Maria was furious. I couldn't believe it either. But clearly deep down in the depths of my subconscious, I had inclinations to get high because I convinced her that I would be able to handle holding the prescription and dosing it out to myself. I enjoyed the high I got from ingesting a couple of them the first night so much that I finished the whole bottle within four days and found myself on the internet trying to contact people to buy more.

In active addiction, I would go to any length to obtain whatever drug I was using. There was almost nothing I wouldn't do. I was known to walk or ride a bicycle twenty miles to the city just to cop heroin if I didn't have enough money to catch a ride. I would spend day and night coming up with schemes to get money to buy drugs. I would lie, manipulate, steal, rob, and hurt people to get what I needed for my fix. This means that if I want to stay clean, I must do the opposite.

I needed to give my maximum effort to protect myself and to put myself as far away from temptation as possible. Maria was an innocent bystander who was in way too deep with me. Maybe she knew better, but I was a master manipulator and rationalizer, so when I said I would be okay holding that bottle of painkillers and dosing it out accordingly, I probably sounded pretty convincing. I also started out with good intentions, but good intentions are no match for the mind games of an addict. Narcotic painkillers should be an absolute very last resort for a recovering addict, and if they are serious about their recovery, they should be taken for as brief of a time period as possible. An addict, by no means, should ever have the power to dispense their own narcotics to themselves. They need someone to oversee the dosage and hold them accountable if they want to survive the endeavor with their sanity and sobriety still intact.

As if by some ironic evil twist of fate, an old using buddy of mine that I hadn't seen in five years got a job at Bertucci's, and he was obviously still getting high. At this point, the outcome of this situation is predictable. When he took his break between shifts to run to the city to get heroin, and I was coming up empty handed looking for pain pills, I slipped him a twenty. He came back, and I ran into the bathroom of the restaurant, fired the heroin and fell into its soft abyss. All the feelings rushed back, and it wasn't until I felt them all again that I realized how much I had secretly missed them. I came out of that bathroom and waited tables in a fury of energy, dripping sweat, and feeling no pain. The fervor with which I did my job was tripled when I was high, and I used it as just another excuse to keep getting high. I knew what I was doing was wrong, but the addiction had already spread its roots into my psyche. My body was a mixture of guilt, terror, anxiety, and depression, and the heroin numbed it all each day.

Eventually, while high and feeling guilty, I confessed to Maria about what I had been doing. I promised I would 'fix it' though, and I asked her to just give me time. At one point I even convinced her to drive me down to the city to cop heroin. I started frequenting some old runners of mine down in East Baltimore on a side street called Durham Street. For now, I could afford to pay them an extra couple dollars to go score for me while I waited in the safety of their row home, away from police and stick up boys. I wasn't the same old guy who used to be in these streets scavenging for money to buy heroin. At this point in time, I had a little muscle, a glow in my skin, jewelry, decent clothes, and a car. Still, I was just a dressed up dope fiend.

I remember pulling up on the strip with gangster music blaring, hopping out with my chain swinging, pants sagging, and an attitude like I was somebody important there. In reality, I was begging to get shot or robbed. Luckily neither happened. I was accepted, probably because I was helping to keep their little economy thriving. I also drew the attention of a rather large woman who ran a dope shop on that street. She thought I was attractive, which earned me occasional free pills whenever I would see her and it guaranteed my protection on that street. I hung out on that street every day, and worked the restaurant at night for a couple of weeks.

I was highly uncomfortable on the inside though. I didn't get the chance to feel any symptoms of heroin withdrawal because I had money and a car to keep the habit running smoothly, however I knew there was a better life for me. The seeds of recovery had already been planted in me many times over. Once a taste of recovery has been felt, and all the knowledge of addiction and recovery has been gained, it ruins your high. The saying 'ignorance is bliss' holds well in this situation. Getting high without the knowledge of how to live a successful life in recovery is painful enough, but it's not as bad when you believe and accept that you are doomed for death and destruction and have no way out. However, once you've learned better and know you can do better, and there is a way out, it makes using drugs much harder because the feelings of guilt and failure that go along with it eat you alive.

Maria, was beginning to lose faith this was just a speed bump in my journey that I would quickly pass over. She finally did what she should have done from the beginning. She told my parents. Everybody was strangely understanding of it all though, and that is because we had a scapegoat. The oral surgeon was to blame, "It wasn't Danny's fault, it was that horrible oral surgeon's!" I was eager to embrace the pity party for once, and the sympathy that came with it. The truth is the doctor could have handled the situation much better, but ultimately I am responsible for every negative thing that happens to me. I didn't have to fill that prescription. I didn't have to keep all fourteen days worth. I didn't have to insist on dispensing them to myself. I should have communicated way before things got out of hand that I was abusing the pills. Also, had I been working a program of recovery as advised by the twelve steps or any spiritual program, I would have had some sort of sponsor or mentor with which to communicate and hold me accountable. I was too early in my recovery journey to understand these things though, and so it was much too easy for me to pass the responsibility onto someone else.

We agreed I needed help. I had almost four years clean and had only been getting high for a couple weeks. A detox probably wasn't necessary; however, my mind is a very tricky mechanism and would convince me I couldn't get clean without it. It also served as an excuse to get high for a couple more days until an appointment was set. The local health department had an outpatient drug program, and I was able to set an appointment with a doctor two days out to begin a plan to detox. That night I was home when Maria got off work from

Bertucci's, and I asked her to come pick me up to go get some ice cream. What happened next is still completely inexplicable. It's as if it was all planned.

We got on the highway about a mile away from the house, and a police car came up behind us and turned their lights on. We pulled over, and the officer asked to see her license, stating he had pulled her over because the light was out above her license plate. I relaxed, nodding out in the passenger seat, completely unconcerned about the interaction. When the officer returned to the car, he asked her if she had any drugs or weapons in the vehicle. When she said "no," he asked if he could search the car.

"Sure, no problem," she replied.

I panicked. "You can say no! Why would you say that?" I whispered to her as we were about to step out of the car. I had a pill of heroin in my pocket. I never in a million years thought our ice cream run would turn into this.

Almost as if it were planned, the officer approached me, and said, "You got anything in your pockets that I should know about?" as he put on rubber gloves. He then ordered me against the vehicle, and he ran his hands over the outside of my jean pockets, feeling every item in them through the denim fabric. My mind was racing. He was deliberately searching for something. He pinched the capsule of heroin through the fabric and with a proud voice of someone who had just found what they were looking for, he said, "Well, well, what's this?" I didn't reply. So he reached in and fished out the pill, then the other contents of my pocket, and he placed them all on the roof of her vehicle with another proud exclamation, "Looks like you're not going home tonight."

I started panicking. "Maria, what's going on?" I shouted.

This was all too strange. I just knew I was being set up. *He came straight for me.* Maria was a street savvy girl, and a tough one. I had a hard time believing she set me up. *Maybe it was my parents? But why would they put me in this situation if they knew I was getting treatment in two days?* My mind was frantic. I knew I was going to jail, and that's exactly what happened.

Maria was released on the scene because she hadn't committed a crime. Days later she would tell me how traumatized she had been by the interaction. The police apparently grilled her. They asked her if she was "a whore, and wanted to grow up being a loser whore." They told her, "He is a piece of shit junkie, and he will be that way for the rest of his life. Junkies never change." They asked her, "Do you want to be a piece of shit too? Because that's what you are, dating a guy like him," they yelled at her. According to her, they were in her face, bullying her and scaring her. She wasn't the type of woman to scare easily; she'd been through a lot in her life. I was angry, but there was absolutely nothing I could do except grow to make liars out of them all.

I went to the county jail that night and slept there for a day and a half before my bail was posted. It only cost $250 to bail me out, and it wasn't a tough decision for my parents and Maria because they knew I had an appointment with the doctor the next morning. I could quickly repay the money with two shifts at the restaurant. Maria picked me up from jail, and we went back to my parents' house. I recall sitting in my bedroom sober for the first time in weeks, thankful to be home, and thankful to be alive. My nerves had the raw sensitivity of coming off of a couple weeks of opiates, and I embraced Maria and professed my love for her. I felt stronger for her than I ever had before and showed it for the first time.

My feelings had been numbed for a couple weeks, and now I was sensitive and emotional from the bounce back of cold reality after being on heroin. I opened up to her like I never had before and told her things I knew she was longing to hear, but that I also honestly felt for her at that time.

The next day I was dropped off at the health department to see the doctor. After a brief wait, I was called back and he did a full assessment of me. He was an Asian man, probably in his fifties, and I wondered just how many drug addicts he saw day in and day out, week after week. It had to be disturbing to see so many wasted lives come and go through his revolving door. I wasn't sure what to expect from this visit, but his suggestion shocked me.

The doctor looked at me and said, "Mr. McGhee, I would like to get you started immediately on a moderate dose of methadone...."

I was instantly elated. I didn't have to stop getting high after all. Then common sense followed close behind. There was no way I was going down that road again. It's a trap. I knew too well from my previous experience on the methadone program that the addiction and withdrawals were worse than heroin. I knew for some it was a necessary evil, and when I had taken it previously, it had actually improved my life temporarily. However, I had since survived a few years with complete abstinence from all drugs, so there was no way I would agree to go any further down that rabbit hole.

I looked up from thought, "Do you really think that's necessary? I've only been using for a few weeks. I don't want to—"

He cut me off, matter of factly, "Mr. McGhee, you are what we term a severe case, a lifetime addict. You have been

65

on and off for years. You simply cannot live effectively without some form of opiate. If you don't get on something now, you will likely die."

I felt almost pure evil in those words. I knew this was not true. I simply knew it. I saw how they put people on methadone maintenance for the rest of their lives. I had been on the program with people who had been coming to the clinics for forty years. I had already made it almost four years without it. *This doctor is a madman*, I thought to myself. The hair stood up on the back of my neck. This was a crossroads for me. My life could go one of two ways in that very moment. I could get on the methadone and take the easy way out, or…

I found the warrior inside of me—and he was angry. I stood up, and for the first time I felt courageous, "Fuck you. Keep your methadone. I came here for help, not poison." I left the office, walking quickly. I had to get away from there as fast as possible, before the methadone called me back in, before I inadvertently drank it and spiraled into an opiate abyss that I could never climb back out of. That moment of clarity at that fork in the road of my life gave me a newfound strength I hadn't felt in a long time. I called Maria to pick me up. When I got in the car I was wound up. "I'm done. I'm fucking done," I said, "I want to go back to work."

The same general manager at Bertucci's had become close to Maria and I, and she was well aware of my struggle. I came back to work, and I worked the next four days straight. I worked through body pains and cold sweats, even though most of it was probably mental. I had never kicked heroin on the street before, ever. It was not something I even thought I could do. I kept telling myself that this last round had only lasted a few weeks, but that didn't quell the mental games that played out in my head or the physical symptoms, real or imagined, I felt. I stayed so busy, running tables on long shifts, that I intentionally exhausted myself so I would have a chance of sleeping at night. The inability to sleep during heroin withdrawal is by far one of the worst symptoms. I thought if I worked intensely for these long hours, I could force my body to sleep, and it worked. Each day I stayed clean, my self-esteem grew and so did my outlook on life. If I could do this, I could do anything. After a few days clean, I started going back to NA meetings and college, and I started my life over again at the point where I had left off, only now with four less teeth.

As was customary, after being humbled by a situation like that, I toed the line for a month or two. I dove back into meetings, work, the gym, church, and my college courses. I had already started letting my grades slip severely and was quickly becoming disheartened by the whole thing. I struggled, trying to catch up from all of my missed courses, projects, and homework I never completed. I barely managed to squeeze out passing grades in most of my classes that semester. However, there were some classes I aced, like speech.

I was terrified of public speaking. My regular conversational skills were horrible, let alone having to speak in front of crowds. I was always a decent writer though, and I wrote about intense emotional topics such as heroin and its impact on me and some of the people I knew. I told the gruesome story about a young woman I knew in Maryland who had stabbed her mother to death for drug money. The daughter left her mother's body lying in the doorway of her home for two weeks, and she stepped over it as she went in and out of the house every day to steal her belongings to sell so she could get more dope.

I also shared about my friend who was a virgin until she was 21 and was the prettiest girl in her school. I described how she consistently tried to convince me to stop using heroin, then years later got hooked on it herself and ended up getting AIDS from prostituting for money to buy the drug.

The day it was my turn to speak, I got physically ill from the anticipation of being in front of the classroom. It was only a class of about twenty students, all younger than me, and yet I was terrified. I shook, my heart raced as if it would beat out of my chest, and I felt nauseous. I stood in front of that small crowd with my notes shaking in my hand and my voice trembling from nerves. But each time I did, my nervousness was interpreted as an emotional response to the content I was speaking about. As I finished my speech on heroin, the professor arose with tears in her eyes, clapping and praising me, saying it was the best speech she'd heard in her twenty years of teaching. I just wanted to run somewhere and hide, and possibly vomit.

There was only one other place my nerves felt that bad, and that was in the courtroom. Unfortunately, because of my recent arrest, I'd be setting foot back in one of them shortly. I had finally finished out all of my probation with flying colors about a month before my latest drug arrest, and luckily so. The probation I was serving had started in 1998 and lasted until 2004. I had been given a 15-year sentence but had served only a small portion. I had violated the probation twice already. Each time, I averted my sentence by getting drug treatment. When I finally went in front of the circuit court judge after I was clean for a few months, he was sick of seeing my face.

He told me sternly, "I'm not going to give you time today. I'm going to give you enough rope to hang yourself with. I'm going to postpone this case for 90 days, and if you can stay clean and out of trouble for those full 90 days, and I don't think you can, then I'll consider not putting you in jail."

"I promise you I will stay clean and out of trouble, Your Honor," I swore back to him.

"I don't believe you," he said in mock disdain, shaking his head.

I knew his position. I knew he had to scare me. I was already scared, but not just scared, I wanted better for myself. And I knew now I could do it. We left the courtroom that day hopeful and relieved. When I say *we*, I mean my parents, members of the community, church friends, family, my manager from work, me, and many others. I had brought a small army with me, and I also had a stack of letters from important people in my life who couldn't make it. Everyone was supportive of me now that I had shown I could stay clean and live right.

Ninety days later I reappeared in his courtroom with the same small crowd, beaming with pride at my accomplishment of sobriety. I stood when my case was called and presented my case and testimony to the judge. He had reports from my probation officer and all of my negative urinalysis tests in front of him. What he did next, I believe was an act and not from his heart, though I could be wrong. He balled up a piece of paper and threw it in my direction from up on his stand and said, "Mr. McGhee, you're a piece of trash. You've been in and out of my courtroom for years. I'm not going to send you to jail. I'm going to continue your probation today, but I'll tell you right now, when you come back in my courtroom, and I believe you will, I don't care if you bring this whole circus of people in here—I don't care if you bring the whole state of

Maryland in here to vouch for you—I will make sure I give you the maximum sentence! Now go on, get out of my sight!"

I stood up relieved. Him throwing the paper ball at me did shock me, but his words meant nothing to me. I felt kind of kindred likability and understanding with him, in spite of the presentation he just delivered. I took his words seriously, but not his emotional outburst. As we exited the courtroom, we were excited, and I was being congratulated and prayed over. My family and church family were aghast at what they had just seen though.

"What an asshole!" "He's really out to get you!" "He doesn't like you at all," were some of the things they said.

"He has to do that," I told them, "He wants to scare me." I explained, "If he didn't like me, he could have easily sent me to jail."

I left the courthouse with three more years of probation, and I made every appointment, passed every drug test, and paid all of my fines on time. Three years later, I finally celebrated completing probation and being out from under the thumb of the law for the first time in almost a decade, and then a month later is when I was pulled over in the car with Maria.

In the gym I was frustrated because I was working out and working hard every day for years now, and yet I was one of the smaller guys in the gym. Instead of working out to be healthy, I was working out to gain other people's respect for me. I had a competitive nature and an ego that told me I had to excel and be one of the best at everything I tried.

I wasn't genetically equipped to be a big guy, so it was something I eventually forced on myself unnaturally. Some old associates of mine and old schoolmates were either members or employees at the gym where I worked out. After asking around a bit, I soon came to realize that almost every guy in my gym was taking steroids. It was like the secret club that no one talked about unless you were a member. I started obsessing over the idea of taking steroids. I was on the internet day and night researching and learning as much as I could. Everything I read had said sixty days was a suggested cycle, and after that you needed to give your body a rest so it could return to homeostasis before doing another cycle, maybe a couple months later. Once I felt content in my knowledge, I contacted a guy in the gym, purchased a couple different products from him, and eagerly started injecting them. I took these two steroids without a real plan and just ate everything I came across for sixty days. It worked like a charm. I blew up like a balloon, gaining over forty pounds and increasing massively in strength.

At the end of sixty days, I was very happy with my results, but I wanted more. I stopped as suggested, but not for long. I set a date for three months out before I began my next cycle, but I got impatient and ended up beginning again within a few weeks. I looked terrible. I went from a naturally lean, healthy young man to an extremely unhealthy barrel-shaped animal. My cheeks filled out and were puffy, and so were my muscles. I thought I looked great though, and so I gained more. I went from 165 pounds before steroids to almost 250 pounds within the first six months. I felt like a new man, and I loved the attention I got from my size. I was so wrapped up in my new obsession that I didn't realize just how bad I looked. My ego was fed daily from remarks people made about my growth and the gains I saw in my strength.

The steroids did not bring about any anger in me, as I often heard they did in others. However, they definitely increased my sex drive. Maria suffered through the whole thing because now my ego and my lust were in overdrive, and there was no way one woman could fill it. She was more than enough for a healthy, emotionally secure man, but I was neither. I was now not only controlled by my ego but also by a testosterone fueled lust that had me sleeping with any woman I would come across. I believed so strongly in my own twisted mind that I was so special and important that I managed to convince Maria and others around me to temporarily believe the same thing. I know she knew what I was up to with these other women, but to lessen the hurt on her heart, it was easier for her to turn a blind eye and try not to catch me.

The gym and sneaking around with women took precedence over all else, and college quickly fell to the wayside. I had missed so many classes and assignments I finally just gave up and stopped going. I had wasted two semesters and almost twenty thousand in student loans for nothing. I partially justified dropping out with two reasons, and although they weren't the entire basis for it, they were definitely motivating factors. The first was money. I had learned what chemical dependency counselors average starting salary was, and it practically broke my heart. Why would I go to school for four years, accrue a ton of debt, and get out only to have a career earning about the same amount of money I was making in the restaurant. I mean, I had made that much money selling cocaine at 16 years old. It was very disheartening. Of course, I wanted to fulfill a greater purpose, and I felt like teaching others from my journey and experiences would be the way to do that, but I just wasn't ready. I was too scared to tap into that part of my past and be around those kinds of people and situations again, to expose myself to feeling those emotions again. I had tried to help a few friends and acquaintances in early recovery, and to watch them get well then relapse took a massive toll on me emotionally. To try to teach someone and give them advice, only to watch them not heed it, then die from a drug overdose broke me. "I'm an emotional dude. I just can't handle all of the sadness, and relapses, and lies," I would rationalize to people when explaining why I didn't follow through with a counseling career. This was partly true. The painful truth was that this had become a defense mechanism because deep down inside, I wasn't ready, I wasn't ready to face that lifestyle again from the other side. Most of all though, I wasn't ready to face myself. I had been avoiding myself for so long. Much like I had done as a child, I was investing my time building walls to hide my true self, rather than face him.

As always, I became obsessed with my hobbies, and at this time my hobbies were steroids and the gym. I would research steroids of all the different types, brands, and prices at night on the internet. There were several sites to buy from online from other countries where they were legal, and I could get them shipped to the Unites States in discreet packaging. The problem was that some of these sites were scams, and the legit ones were very costly and took a long time to ship. I had a wild idea one night and checked eBay. To my surprise there wasn't the wider known Anabolic steroids on there, but there were some illegal prescription fat burners. I placed an order just out of curiosity and sure enough, it showed up at my house a few days later. I then sent the seller a private email and told him if he had any other products he wasn't able to list on eBay, that I'd be interested. He responded with a long list of products at extremely cheap prices. I had hit a goldmine!

I placed one order, and then another. I placed a few more orders until I had a stockpile. I was getting products for $18 that I could sell for $100 in the gym, or fat burners for $8 that I could sell for $40 to women I knew. The markups were incredible to me. Right there, in the basement of my parents' house, in my father's home real estate office, my new hustle was born. I began supplying the gym. I was doing what I did best and what I loved. I started ordering so much that I began driving to New Jersey to meet my supplier face to face. He was a doctor of Bulgarian decent from New York. I never understood why a doctor would go through eight years of schooling and have the potential to make an amazing income, and risk it all for a few dollars on the side. Nevertheless, I knew it happened every day in America. I didn't question him; he was my new friend. I had a newfound feeling of importance as I supplied fat burners to most of the women at the restaurant and steroids to some of my coworkers. I had a large list of clientele in my gym and other gyms. I was supplying people in gyms all across the city and hand delivering them myself. I had police and correctional officers on my clientele list. When I was at work at the restaurant, some of my customers would come in, and I would put their steroids in a small pizza box and hand it off to them in the front of the restaurant or out of the back door. On quite a few occasions, I had officers come in the lobby or pull up at the backdoor to get their goods. My coworkers who were in on my new business were astonished at what was going on.

One is too many and a thousand is never enough. This is a common saying in the rooms of the twelve step programs and is as old as the programs themselves. It applies to an addict's insatiable desire for the drugs and alcohol and its ability to destroy you with just one use. The problem with addiction, as I've said earlier, is that the drugs are only a symptom of an underlying personality defect, so when the drugs are removed, something else inevitably takes their place. This is only if the underlying personality defect goes unappreciated and untreated. I had now become addicted to the money and the importance I felt of supplying a need. Since the desire was insatiable, I was never satisfied and constantly sought to take it to new heights, no matter the risk or how insane. I knew almost everyone at my job smoked marijuana except me. It suddenly made sense to me that since I now had extra money to give me purchasing power, and I had a need to fill, that I should take advantage of this new opportunity.

I never liked marijuana. I had tried smoking it several times throughout my teenage years. It usually ended with me having full blown panic attacks, only I didn't know they were panic attacks. I had no clue what was wrong with me. I knew almost all of my friends grew up smoking marijuana regularly. They swore by it, saying it relaxed them and made their life seemingly much more enjoyable. When I would occasionally try it, I would end up hiding in a bathroom somewhere with heart palpitations, scared to death, and praying to God to make the feelings go away. Since I couldn't enjoy the drug all of my coworkers seemed to love, I rationalized I should make some money off of it. I also rationalized, that while it was illegal, it wasn't addictive, so I wouldn't be jeopardizing my morals or my recovery by selling it. It was natural, it was safe, and it wasn't hurting anyone.

I bought a pound of weed at a time and broke it down into smaller increments and made some extra money. I operated with extreme paranoia and precaution. I knew if I got caught selling illegal drugs I was done. This is the sheer insanity of it all. My criminal record was extensive because of my addiction. Selling marijuana could have landed me with an extremely long sentence in prison because of my record, and yet I risked it all for a couple more dollars and some ego-filling feelings of importance. I also risked my only place to live by keeping it tucked away in my closet in my parents' house, where they were allowing me to live at the age of 25 years old now. I was clean, but I definitely hadn't grown up or worked on any aspect of my recovery.

I still sat in NA meetings a couple of days a week and went through the motions; pretending I was doing what I was supposed to be doing. I was mainly in there looking at females and counting down the minutes until it was time to leave. My court date for the possession charge in the car with Maria came and went, and I was given probation because I had completed all of my necessary drug counseling and urine screenings successfully. I was back on probation, but unconcerned because I was clean and knew I would continue to pass my drug tests and see my agent on time. As long as I was extremely careful, I would be okay, I convinced myself.

I met a stripper online. I hung out with her outside of work, and she bought some of the clenbuterol I was selling. Before long the other strippers at her work were asking for it. I found myself going to the strip club on the outskirts of Baltimore and hanging out during the day when I dropped off boxes of these pills. Now my ego was in full bloom. While the other men in the club were drooling and throwing money at these women, I was uninterested in their sexuality; I wanted their money. It was ego-fueling for me to show up like a hot shot and watch them collect money from other men and then spend it with me. Like a good addict with an insatiable desire for more, it didn't stop there. When one of them asked me if I could get some coke, I said sure.

The spiral always starts to spin faster the deeper you go. It begins with one bad idea, one that's not too bad, and then one bad idea slowly turns into an even worse one over time. Then bad ideas start to pile on top of each other, still getting increasingly worse until you've lost all discernment of what's good or bad anymore. At some point you let go of the control you never really had, and you just let the momentum of your spiral take you down. The amount of steroids I was getting from the doctor in New York had surpassed anything he could get on hand, so he started having his family members in Bulgaria ship it to me directly. I would get big boxes labeled 'American Eagle Clothing' shipped directly to my parents' house, only they were full of vials and bottles of pills. I was still supplying my coworkers and a few people outside of work with marijuana, and I had reconnected with an old friend in West Baltimore and started to get ounces of cocaine.

I was pulling up at the NA meetings, drinking coffee, smoking cigarettes, and talking recovery while I had a trunk full of drugs in my car out in the parking lot. In my mind, I was a good man though. *I have morals*, I'd convince myself. I would never sell to anyone in the meetings or even let them know what I was doing because I didn't want to jeopardize anyone's recovery. I had each foot planted in two completely contradictory worlds, and I was straddling a fence that could potentially sever me in half. The hypocrisy of it all should have driven me insane, but the hustle fueled my obsession and kept me motivated. As long as I have an obsession to focus all of my energy on, then it is like a defense mechanism to push reality aside, which in turn keeps my anxiety and depression at bay. The untreated part of my spiritual disease is what I am burying by focusing on an obsession. As I've said before, and will continue to repeat, drugs and alcohol along with any other obsession are only symptoms of a greater underlying spiritual disease. As long as the spiritual affliction goes untreated, it will continually be replaced by a physical and/or psychological addiction.

Now, I was selling steroids, cocaine, and marijuana while clean. In one sense this was walking a very tricky line that brought me dangerously close to using, but in another sense it built yet another wall between me and using. It built a fragile wall of ego that, once again, made me think I was a big shot and better than the addicts. I stayed away from heroin and alcohol, because I believed those were my only problems. There was no way in my mind I could go back to using drugs because I was too tough for that. I had no clue how dangerously close I really was.

I ran into an old face at the strip club where I was selling cocaine. It was Manny, who I had attended Second Genesis Treatment Center with several years prior. He was one of the many guys who had pretended to be an addict in order to beat a prison sentence by going to a treatment center to avoid a long jail time. He had been a headache for me inside of the program. He was one of the people who had outed me for sleeping with one of the women inside of the treatment program, all the while he was selling cocaine during his stay in the program and sleeping with one of the counselors. There was a lot of corruption in that facility, and unfortunately, I bore much of the brunt of it. I was eventually thrown out and told to wait on the bus to go back to prison, but I climbed out of the window and went on the run instead. On one hand I had a little bit of resentment against Manny because of the part he played in my being sent back to prison, but on another hand, I looked up to him because of his drug dealing status and connections on the street. I knew Manny ran with some serious guys in East Baltimore and had moved a lot of weight. I knew he had never retired from selling cocaine because when one of the graduates of Second Genesis was found dead from a drug overdose in an alley in East Baltimore, Manny's number came up in his cell phone as the last person he had called. Manny was a younger Black guy known to sell drugs. The man who had overdosed was an old White guy known to use them. It wasn't hard to put two and two together.

When we ran into each other in the strip club that afternoon, it was like an old reunion, all smiles and hugs. He was obviously doing well. I noticed immediately the gold and diamond rings and the chunky diamond bracelet on his wrist. He was amazed at my transformation and size and the brand name clothes and jewelry I wore. We both knew what each other was up to without having to say it. He told me he was dating one of the strippers who danced there and not to worry because he wasn't hustling inside of the club—meaning, he wasn't going to step on my toes and compete for clientele in there. He said he was only selling ounces or more, and if I wanted to, I could call him anytime to buy ounces of cocaine for cheap. We traded numbers and chatted for a bit. I tucked his number away, just in case, although I still didn't trust him. That was the last time I saw him there.

I had been traveling to the other side of the city about once a week to see a Black woman I was dating behind Maria's back. Ironically, she was a West Baltimore police officer. She lived in the Baltimore Highlands just outside of the city. I would hang at her house and watch movies, and she would have me sell weed to people in her neighborhood. At the time just the fact that I was sleeping with a police officer and selling drugs out of her house made me feel even more important. My ego was inflated by things that truly didn't matter, but in the context of my immature mindset, they meant everything, it gave me self-imagined power and bragging rights. It took one strange late night at her house for everything to change. We were watching a movie, and I began trying to get sexual with her, but she was completely unreceptive to my advances. The more I tried, the angrier she got.

Finally in a fit of anger, she stripped off her clothes and said, "Is this what you want? Come on, fuck me then!"

Of course, her outburst had the opposite effect on me. I quickly felt awkward, and I shriveled up inside, feeling like an ingrate. She wouldn't tell me what was wrong, though I continued to plead with her to talk to me.

"Just fuck me! That's what you want, right? Come on, just fuck me."

I couldn't. I tried, but I couldn't. The scene had become anything but sexual or seductive. I knew she was hurting, and I was so blind I couldn't see why. In my mind our situation was normal; what we were doing was just for fun. It was okay to just come over once a week behind my girlfriend's back to fuel my little ego and leave. But she was finally done being used. I could sense it, but she wouldn't say it. Finally, after going back and forth with each other, she laid down a new law.

"You're not coming over here and fucking me anymore unless you're staying the night!"

She had me. For me, that was unheard of. I hadn't stayed

the night at a woman's house since my drinking days, and the only reason I did then was because I was either too drunk to get out of bed, or I had nowhere to go. There was an uncomfortable dose of reality waking up next to a woman that I wasn't prepared for. I shouldn't have been sleeping with a woman if I wasn't prepared to wake up to her, but at that time it was only for my ego. I didn't understand anything except my own selfish desires. So when she presented me with an ultimatum, it left my mind spinning, confused, and upset. I left her house quietly and drove off into the night, not knowing who I was or why I did anything that I did.

As I had done many times before, I drove the hour drive home up I-95 with the windows down and the cool night air blowing in as the music played. I drove past the lights and buildings of Baltimore City, past all of the exits for the west side, and I went through the tunnel. I was just about to pass the city when I had an awful idea. I had a broken and unfulfilled ego, and the night was young. I knew a strip on the Eastside of Baltimore where I could pick up a prostitute and get a blowjob for twenty dollars. This is what I had gotten clean for. This was my new way of life. I, of course, didn't look at the ridiculousness of it all when I was doing it because I had my blinders on. I was caught up in the moment, in the ego trap I was living in. The only thing I was focused on was self-fulfillment in order to put a band-aid on the brokenness inside of me. Driving through the city looking for a prostitute at night isn't much different than driving through the city looking for drugs, motivated with the excitement of driving up one street and down another until I found the means I was looking for to escape myself.

I did this about three times over the next week. I could

have gotten sexual satisfaction from Maria or somewhere else, but like the drugs, the thrill of the hunt made it more exciting. The thing is, the prostitutes were supplying my need to fill my ego and its insatiable desire, and I in turn gave them money to fulfill their need for drugs to do the same. It all boils back down to a spiritual disease eating away at our souls. I was still spiraling further into darkness. The more I thought about these women shooting their cocaine and heroin, and the more I was coming to these neighborhoods of East Baltimore for illicit activity, the more the old junkie-mentality started to set in. Heroin started becoming very tempting again. I felt the obsession brewing inside of me—and somehow, I stopped it. I caught myself. For once, I caught myself before it was too late. Like a splash of cold water to my face, those thoughts gave me a reality check, and I made instant changes.

It was the sudden realization that I wasn't building myself up. Rather, my ego was actually destroying me. I unloaded the last of the cocaine and marijuana and never replenished my stock. I was done going to West Baltimore to see my female friend over there; in fact, we never spoke again. I was done with the prostitutes and done selling drugs. I felt myself falling, and somehow by the grace of God, I was strong enough to catch myself on the way down. This was a turning point. I didn't know it at that time, but this was the end of my self-destruction and the beginning of a massive cycle of growth. A cycle of growth that started with a very slow crawl, but inevitably took me to a place higher than I ever imagined.

LEVEL THREE

I've got a bad disease
Out from my brain is where I bleed
Insanity it seems
Has got me by my soul to squeeze

—Red Hot Chili Peppers

I'VE ALWAYS HAD vast creative energy, and even though I'm not a musician or an artist, I'm a thinker and a writer. Unfortunately, creative thinking has led me into most of my troubles in life. I always harnessed it for negative purposes. I easily concocted ways to make money illegally, break the law, or get whatever I wanted without actually working for it. The problem for me became that my talents no longer served me in my recovered life.

With the exception of using and selling steroids, I had let go of all other illegal dealings at this point. I didn't consider steroids to be an illicit drug and rationalized to myself that they were almost borderline legal, even though I had to have them discreetly mailed to me from other countries, then sell them behind closed doors and out of sight. I was making decent money between working my side hustle and waiting tables. Maria and I were going strong, although I was still sneaking around with other women occasionally. I knew I had to slow my steroid use and give my body time to recuperate, so I had taken a couple months off from using and was only selling them. All was good in the world. I was living in the present and ignoring the inevitable future. I was somehow staying clean and living life one day at a time, but I knew there had to be more to life. And there certainly was more, it was just a lot worse than I ever expected.

One random spring morning I awoke and walked out onto my parents' back deck to smoke my first morning cigarette. As was my routine, I took pulls off of the cigarette and looked out into the forest behind their house, only I suddenly became hyper aware. For no apparent reason, reality was suddenly sharpened by one thousand percent, and panic took hold of my entire body. My skin started heating up, and gloom clouded over my brain. I searched and scrambled for a way out, but I couldn't begin to find a way. The feelings intensified. I was in a peaceful, serene setting on an average day, yet my body was stricken with extreme panic. The entire universe was huddled together, staring at me, and telling me how worthless and pointless I was, that there was absolutely zero reason for my existence, and that I was a burden on the world around me. My heart palpitated, my organs stop in place, and my skin crawled and pulsated. I staggered inside and yelled out, but neither one of my parents were home.

At 26 years old, I collapsed onto their sofa and buried my head into a pillow, however my body kept racing as if I was running a marathon. I couldn't just lay there. I got up to move, but my body was almost frozen in place. Every single thought, every action, even the idea of thinking sent electric shocks of fear that trembled through my body. I had been in fist fights, gotten shot at, and lived through overdoses, prison, car wrecks and more, and I had never been so scared. *And for what?* There was nothing to be scared of, and still gripping, relentless fear had overcome me. I made my way to the cordless phone, ripped it from its cradle, and called my mother. When she picked up and I blurted out, "I don't know what's wrong with me. Something is seriously wrong with me. I can't explain it, but I can't live like this." Tears poured from my eyes. Fear had me in its clutches, and the symptoms were ungodly real.

"Calm down, you're having a panic attack. You've been through this before. Just breathe." My mother said matter of factly into the phone.

She was right, I had had many panic attacks in my life. It took me a long time to realize what they were. They had been with me since I was about 16. At first, they only happened when I smoked marijuana. After only one or two hits I'd find myself hiding in the bathroom feeling strange bubbles under my rib cage as if I needed to burp, only I couldn't. The bubbles would expand and contract, and then rise into my chest and cause me to panic. Irrational fears would overcome my body, and I would begin praying fervently to God to take my high away. Only time would cure it, and I would avoid my friends while taking deep breaths, trying to calm myself down.

Then in my late teens, I started having similar experiences while sober in between bouts of drinking. My heart would race and palpitate for no reason, and I would become hyper aware. I would develop sharp stabbing pains around my heart, and my left arm would go numb. They felt so real, so terrifying, that I went to the emergency room on three separate occasions swearing I was in the midst of a heart attack. No matter how many professionals diagnosed them as panic attacks, I would argue that the physical sensations were way too real, and it had to be something else. Around the age of 18, after several of these episodes, I was given an EKG, a stress test for my heart, and a Holter monitor, and they all reported that my heart health was fine. In my mind at that time, I would have preferred there had been an actual issue with my heart rather than some phantom illness that no one seemed to believe or understand. This in turn fueled my fire to drink more and more often and eventually to use heroin in the same capacity. As long as I was under the influence, I couldn't feel those feelings as strongly, although they did sometimes try to creep in on my heroin high.

As I continued into my years of drug use, the anxiety attacks came back full force particularly when I was on methadone. By that time, I had finally accepted them for what they were. While on methadone, the doctor at the clinic had put me on a prescription for Ativan that worked wonders. However, Ativan, Xanax, and Klonopin, which are the normal medications taken for panic attacks and severe anxiety, are also highly addictive mind-altering drugs. Once I was in recovery, I knew I absolutely could not take these benzodiazepines because I would definitely abuse them and become reliant on them to function. I knew enough about myself to understand that.

Cringing through one of my typical panic attacks head-on with no medication was torturous enough, but what I went through that morning was on a level of pure hell I can't even begin to describe. From what I had researched, the average person's panic attack lasts about 20 minutes. Mine generally lasted an hour or two, just long enough for me to be seen in the emergency room, and by the time the doctor would get to me, I had generally returned to normal. Not this time. The panic attack that began on my parents' deck was on a whole different level. It lasted almost three weeks straight.

To cover the various feelings of terror and thresholds of fear I crossed in my mind, along with the horrific bodily sensations would take a book in and of itself. Accompany that with the complete inability to sleep or function on any sort of level, and you get the picture of what a disaster my mental and physical state of being became. I spent the majority of the first week and a half wide-eyed, clutching a pillow against my chest, crying, and wishing for death. I called on God more than I ever had before, even in the throes of my active addiction. It was the worst torture I had ever endured, and with each new day, it was still there, only worse. It was one thing when I had anxiety attacks I could trace back to a drug or alcohol, but this never-ending bout of terror came without explanation. I ran through my thoughts over and over again trying to pinpoint a cause, but I could find none. The steroids had been out of my system for way too long. I had been drug and alcohol free. I was regularly taking my Paxil as prescribed for anxiety. There was no evident explanation for why they came at this point in my life, or why they came at all.

Maria was by my side throughout the whole ordeal. She too suffered occasional but severe anxiety attacks and understood me on that level, but she had never suffered one longer than 20 minutes or had one of this intensity. It completely crippled me. She was very loving and supportive, and every day I looked forward to her coming to my parents' house when she got off of work and comforting me. It was a minuscule amount of comfort compared to the hell I was experiencing, but every little bit helped me to feel somewhat human and worthwhile. Watching movies with her at night on my parents' couch, trying to distract my mind from the horrors within, was maybe the only time I didn't feel suicidal, as the terrors would calm enough to let me sit still.

Then in bed, I would toss and turn for hours through the night listening to my heart beat rapidly, as I prayed and cried. My fear of falling asleep was that I would wake up in the morning refreshed and the terror would come racing back in and all of the bodily sensations that came with it. I would pray to God, begging Him to take it away, and to please make me normal when I awoke in the morning. But every morning, after finally getting a couple hours of sleep, I would awake before the rest of the world wide-eyed, alert, and terror stricken. As my eyes would crack open, my first thoughts would be, "Please God, no. Please let it be over," but it all come rushing back. My pulse quickened. My skin felt electric and on fire, and the whole universe seemed to zero in on me, right there alone at 4 or 5 AM while the rest of the world slept. It is a lonely, scary hour of the day when the world is seemingly in limbo but you are being spun recklessly on a carousel of terror that shows no sign of stopping. I wanted to die often during those weeks of terror. Death felt like the only reprieve from the feelings of sheer panic, pointlessness, hopelessness, and misery that strangled my soul. I wished for death but knew it would never come simply by wishing for it.

There was one thing I knew could make these feelings go away. It was absolutely the most simple solution, and it was created specifically for situations like mine, and that was benzodiazepines. Almost every woman I knew carried Xanax in their purse in case of emergency. I knew for a fact Maria had some that her mother had given to her for anxiety attacks. I was pretty sure my mother had some stashed away as well. I knew it would rescue me from the unrelenting mental and physical torture as surely as I knew gravity held me on this Earth. I knew with every fiber in my being that one Xanax, Klonopin, or Valium could make all the panic and terror go away. I would rather have been brutally beaten from the time I woke up to the time I went to sleep than to feel the inner terror and anxiety and the physical sensations that go with it.

I wished for death daily, and yet I would not take the only immediate cure I knew of. I stood firm in my belief that Xanax, or any of its relatives, were the low hanging fruit that would open up a world of misery, which would not only destroy me, but possibly cause more hurt for those around me.

Somewhere, somehow in the midst of my greatest darkness and misery, I found the warrior within. It was as if I was living in abject poverty and destitution my whole life, starving and barely staying alive, and I knew where I could easily find a bag with ten million dollars in it. Yet I chose not to. I chose not to take the easy way out because I knew I would never grow from that. If I took the easy way out, I would not learn or grow from my decision. Instead, I would disappoint myself. I would be cloaked in guilt, and I would have to rely on more Xanax, or benzodiazepines, in order to keep the feelings at bay. And thus, I would start the cycle of addiction all over again.

In my greatest moments of weakness and feelings of worthlessness, I found my biggest growth. I wouldn't realize this for many years, but the fact that I didn't reach out and take the readily available cure for my insanity and inner torture is beyond amazing. I still knew, somehow, lost in that oblivion of hopelessness that I had a bigger purpose. The only thing I could hope for was that time would slowly start to pull me out of it.

The United States has such a huge mental health crisis that when someone has a breakdown like this there are literally lines ahead of them to get help. I had no health insurance. I reached out to local crisis clinics and counselors, even the local health department, and everyone was backed up for months. I literally felt like I couldn't survive another minute in my own head. I was physically shaking, crying, and wishing for nothing but sweet death to rescue me. Yet every time I called someone and notified them of my situation, they couldn't schedule an appointment for me for at least a month or two out. I knew from prior experience that the emergency room wouldn't do anything except recommend a psychologist, who would then make me wait a long while for an appointment. I wasn't in the frame of mind to pick up a phone and dial anyone. It sounds completely insane, but my irrational fear had every cell in my body under its control. The idea of picking up a phone to call someone seemed as scary as sky diving without a parachute. I had Maria or my parents make the calls when they were available.

I was going to have to go to the local hospital and tell them I wanted to kill myself in order to be admitted and get immediate treatment. That was the only solution I knew of. I didn't really want to kill myself, but I did want to die. I only wanted to die to escape the torture I was entrapped in. What I really wanted was for the torture to go away and to remain alive. I knew, however, that the only way to get immediate intake into a hospital was by threatening suicide or attempting it. It was also a common trick addicts used during active addiction in order to get off of the streets and get a couple days of reprieve and treatment. The most obvious hospital in the area to call first was a nearby mental health institution called Sheppard Pratt. My father called them to find out what their intake process was like. They informed him that if I wasn't an imminent danger to myself or others, that there was another option available called 'Day Hospital' a two-week program where I would be dropped off at 8 AM in and picked up at 3:30 PM Monday through Friday. The only other 'option' was the suicidal route. I agreed to try the Day Hospital. Maria, being the perfect girlfriend to her entirely flawed boyfriend agreed to drive me back and forth every single day while still working the restaurant fulltime. A benefit of having an entirely open and honest relationship with my employer was that not only were they understanding and sympathetic to what was happening to me, but they were willing to welcome me back when I got better. They would often send their regards and well wishes with Maria.

I felt like such a burden on Maria and on my family once again, and now I had no real explanation why. At least before, I could blame it on the drugs and alcohol. Now it just felt like pure cowardice and weakness. The only thing I could do was try my best to get better and get normal and show my appreciation for them all. It humbled me. I didn't realize it then, and in fact I didn't realize it until many years later, but my anxiety and depression kept me in check. They kept my pride and my ego from growing out of control. They were the ultimate tag team that could appear out of nowhere and break me as quickly as they wanted. This, I realized eventually, was a blessing inside of a curse. The only thing I knew at that moment was that I had to pull through for those who had stood by me. I simply couldn't let them down.

The Day Hospital lasted two weeks, and those two weeks flew by. The schedule consisted of groups all day long intermixed with occasional one-on-one meetings with assigned counselors. It really did nothing to change my thinking patterns or introduce me to new coping techniques I hadn't already learned. Honestly, the most valuable thing it gave me was structure and a safe place to stay busy until the panic and depression eventually subsided. With each passing day the terror regressed to a point that I could eventually function normally. All I really needed was time, but there was no way I could have successfully spent those hours alone in my parents' house while the rest of the world worked. Being alone and feeling hopeless while fighting the demons inside was much harder than doing it within the structured schedule of the Day Hospital.

Finally, I was able to return to work, and life quickly fell back into a comfortable rhythm. The anxiety and depression became a thing of the past almost as quickly as it had come into existence. It was random and unfounded, but it humbled me. I never wanted to feel that way again. I walked through life on eggshells praying it would never return.

I started doing everything I could to prevent those feelings from coming back. Since I had no idea what caused them, I decided to just stop doing anything I considered to be 'not living right'. I stopped sleeping with random women behind Maria's back. I stopped using steroids. I started going back to Narcotics Anonymous meetings and church. I had no idea what was wrong with me, so I changed my behavior just in case one of those behaviors had been a trigger. The one thing I didn't stop was selling steroids, and that quickly came back to bite me.

Manny had called me about two months back when I had stopped selling cocaine to see if I could get him any weight in coke for around the same price he was getting it for. He told me his connection had just disappeared and he was afraid he had either gotten locked up or fled the country. I explained to him that I was out of that game and didn't have anyone to call to get some. I could have found it if I wanted to, but I didn't want to get back into the drug trade. We hung up on good terms. Then I heard from him about a month later.

"Hey yo, you still got the thing you was doing? I got some guys coming in from out of town looking to get about thirty pounds of that good dro."

I hesitated for a second and said, "Naw bro, that dried up. I'll see if I can find anything else."

I had no intention of finding any more weed for him. There was no way I was going to be the middle-man in a drug transaction upwards of seventy thousand dollars between some country white folk and these inner-city gangsters who I knew carried guns. It was a nightmare waiting to happen, and the whole thing sounded an alarm in me. But when Manny called back the third time a couple weeks later, he asked for steroids and I obliged him.

"Aye look bro, you still got them steroids? I'm in the gym now, and I'm trying to get my weight up."

"Sure thing, bro. What you need?" I happily replied, believing this to be a harmless transaction.

I drove back and forth to the city on several occasions spanning a month or two selling him various amounts and types of steroids. Then he called me one sunny afternoon and asked what I had on hand. I was almost out. I had run really low and had considered not having any more mailed to me. I was done looking over my shoulder and living illicitly. The steroid market was flooded at the moment with people ordering their own online, or other people selling in the gyms. So the demand for what I had wasn't as high as it once was. I wasn't going out of my way to look for people to buy it, I was just waiting for them to call me. Since the market had dried up, I figured it was an easy time to get out.

So when Manny called, I only had a couple bottles of testosterone and a couple boxes of clenbuterol left. He asked me to grab the last of the testosterone and meet him at our usual spot in Baltimore County. It was about a thirty-minute ride from my house, and I had a busy afternoon planned. I sped off down the highway with the windows down and music blaring feeling the summer air whipping against me. I exited the highway and took route 43 in White Marsh towards another exit ramp onto Route 40 into the city. As I flew off the exit ramp, I passed a police car on the median. *Shit*, I thought to myself, *I'm definitely getting pulled over.* I was clearly speeding. I stared into the rearview once I passed him waiting for him to pull out and flip on his whirling lights and siren, but nothing happened. *I was extremely lucky*, I thought to myself as I continued onto Route 40.

When I came around the exit there were two unmarked black SUVs driving the wrong way up the exit and they skidded sideways, blocking the street. I crushed my breaks wondering what the hell was going on. As I stopped I glanced at my rearview to see more trucks pull in from the rear. Men hopped out with guns drawn and vests on. They were plain-clothed in jeans and baseball hats, so my first irrational thought was that this was some kind of elaborate robbery. As they swarmed my car demanding I exit with my hands in the air, I realized I was being arrested. *There is no way this is over steroids*, I thought to myself, *maybe they have the wrong guy.* But I was forced at gunpoint to lay in the middle of the street and my name was spoken aloud as cuffs were placed on my wrists. As they crowded me and one of them placed his knee into the middle of my back, I knew I was in serious trouble.

I didn't fight. I didn't argue. I played dumb. "What is this about?" I asked sounding as baffled as I could.

"What's in your car?! Where are the drugs?!" One of them demanded.

"I've got a couple bottles of testosterone in the glove compartment, but no real drugs if that's what you're looking for." I couldn't believe this was happening. I had stopped all my illegal activities. I had given it all up, and here I was on the last couple bottles of steroids, and this was happening. I decided to keep my mouth shut and wait.

I was taken back to the Baltimore County police precinct and placed in a holding cell. An officer came to inform me that my parents' house was being raided at that very moment and once that was finished, they would decide what to do with me.

"Be cooperative with us, and things will work out much better for you," he said.

"Yeah, no problem. What do you need to know?" I replied, acting like this was all silly and no big deal.

"Where are the drugs in your house?"

"Look in my nightstand on the left side of my bed. There are two bottles of testosterone and two boxes of clenbuterol there. That's all I have. I was seriously done. I was done. That's all I have."

He walked off.

I couldn't believe my parents were going through this. What had I done? I was still making their lives a living hell. I imagined them sitting handcuffed on the couch while their house was torn apart and ransacked. I was doomed. I definitely wouldn't have a place to live if I made it out of here without going to jail.

After a couple hours in a holding cell, I was invited back into a room with two detectives sitting at a table.

"We can take you to jail tonight or you can walk out of here free. That is going to depend on you. You've been helpful with us so far, and we appreciate you telling us where the drugs were stashed, but we're going to need a lot more help than that."

"Okay sure, what can I help with?" I asked, already knowing where I was going to take this.

While sitting in the holding cell, I had managed to piece together the events that led me to this place. It was painfully obvious that Manny had set me up. I had coyly remarked to the detectives during the arrest that they were wasting all these resources for steroid possession. And he replied back that they had me on wire surveillance making several sales to a controlled buyer. At first, I had a hard time grasping that it could be Manny because I knew how immersed in the streets he was. I knew he carried guns and sold cocaine and had done prison time. It was ridiculous to think it was him, but he was the only person I had sold to in Baltimore County repeatedly. Every other sale I had made was either done in the city or other counties. Ironically, he was the only person I met in that jurisdiction.

"We need to know who your supplier is. Where are you getting this stuff? Give us that, and you won't go to jail tonight," I was told.

I immediately began blabbing everything I had already rehearsed in my mind. I wasn't going to tell on the doctor from Jersey; I didn't believe in throwing someone else under the bus for my own mistakes. "Do the crime, do the time," was a basic tenet I lived by. I had taken risks, and I had been caught, therefore it was my responsibility to deal with the consequences. I didn't believe in rolling over on other people to save myself, but I did think I had a plan that could benefit me and still wouldn't hurt anyone else.

"I get them off of the internet. There are a bunch of sites I can show you. I'll show you guys all of them, no problem," I responded proudly, while feigning extreme willingness to help.

They probed me a bit more, asking if there was anyone in person that I could possibly lead them to. But I promised them I only ordered off the internet and that was all I could help them with. Eventually they placed me back in the holding cell. Within an hour I was uncuffed and released.

I was given these words before exiting the building: "Your future is in your hands; you can go to jail or you can help us. Sometime soon you will be contacted by someone in our department to show them everything you know. I suggest you tell them everything."

I agreed and walked out of the police station and into the fresh night air. That was a close call. I called Maria to come pick me up and then called my parents, terrified at what their reaction might be. It was surprising to say the least. When they picked up the phone, I braced myself for the rage I expected to follow. However, what I heard in their voices was more relief than anything. The police had been reasonable with my parents and only searched my bedroom, instead of trashing the whole house. Since I told them where the steroids were hidden, they did a quick in-and-out without damaging anything. My parents were shocked at first that I was up to my old tricks, but were actually relieved to find out it was only testosterone and fat burner pills. Based on my history, their initial response to a driveway full of police vehicles was that I must be out robbing and stealing to get drug money again.

My place to stay wasn't compromised, still there was another mark against me when it came to reasons for my parents to push me out of the house. I was 27 years old now but operating on the level of an 18-year-old. I had very little real-world experience sober and was terrified of being out in it alone. I had a complete failure to launch. My parents had raised three children to adults and had earned their peace of mind, only to have their drug addict son return home with no real sign of leaving. On top of that police were still being called to their house years into my supposed sobriety.

The thought of being alone with responsibility and bills was as terrifying as being dropped somewhere in the middle of the ocean to me. I knew the day would inevitably come, but I doubted I would ever be prepared for it. My parents wouldn't let me live there forever, nor did I want to be a burden on them or anyone else. I was my own worst enemy. I had never lived on my own sober. I had never done many things sober; I had no idea how. I had masked reality for so long with drugs and alcohol that all of the little things, especially things I could potentially screw up, were terrifying to me. I had to learn how to interact with women while sober once I got clean. I didn't have my first sober sexual encounter until I was 24 years old. Sure, I had multitudes before that, but they were all under the influence of drugs and alcohol. I still had to learn all the other basics of life, without relying on a chemical crutch. Taking the first steps into normalcy was unnerving. I was ultimately going to need a push.

Failure scared me, but so did success. At my parents' place, I was stuck in a comfortable rut of nothingness. If I experienced success for any period of time, I would manage to self-sabotage my progress because deep down I felt I didn't deserve it. I concluded it was stressful to maintain success and failure was inevitable, so I may as well screw up sooner rather than later in order to avoid the stress. However, if I failed, that was also stressful. If I failed and ended up in the streets with nothing, I was almost sure I would have to use drugs or drink to cope, and that would ultimately become a living hell all over again. These thoughts plagued my mind and left me stagnant, unable to move in any direction.

So as my parents naturally continued to push me out the door with ultimatums, I chose any option that would keep me under their roof longer. When given the ultimatum that I either had to get back into college or move out, I chose to enroll in school, but first I stalled as long as I could.

I continued working at Bertucci's and working out regularly, just without the steroids now. With that hustle gone, I had to find a new one. It didn't take long at all. I was always into urban fashion and followed trends and famous designers. I knew what discount designer brands the shops carried and where to find certain brand names for cheap, as well as what was in demand at the time. When I discovered eBay, I explored the platform and quickly found my niche. I figured out what clothing I could purchase in discount designer stores such as Marshalls, TJ Maxx, Burlington Coat Factory, and the like, then I'd sell it for three times what I paid for it on eBay. There were plenty of people overseas or in the Midwest who didn't have access to urban metropolises and were willing to pay top dollar for these brands. Within weeks I had a full blown store on the auction site and a huge stock, complete with mannequins for taking photos, all in my parents' basement. I knew every store in the tristate area that carried these goods and which ones had the best stocks. I would spend most of my time off work driving to Delaware, Pennsylvania, or near DC to stock up.

I always had to hustle; it was ingrained in me. The problem was I always hustled for the wrong thing. There was never enough money for me because I blew it chasing the wrong things. Instead of saving money for a house or a down payment on an apartment and furnishings, I blew it immediately on things that dressed up the outside of me. I was still much too concerned with building a solid image to protect the weak person inside than actually making common sense plans for the future. In my late twenties, I was still living in my parents' basement without a dime in my bank account, but I looked like a big shot. It's all that mattered to me.

Six months had gone by since the drama on the exit ramp, and I hadn't heard anything from the police regarding a steroid bust. I woke up every day waiting on that hammer to drop. I knew it would come eventually. There was no way they would just let it slide. I tried to go about my daily life, but it always sat in the back of my mind. *Will today be the day?*

When the call finally came, I was both relieved and panicked. It was time to face reality and the consequences of yet another bad decision. The detective on the phone was from Baltimore County, and he proposed we meet up and talk. He also said that since the bust happened in Baltimore County but the house raid happened in Harford County, that I would be meeting up with a detective from Harford as well. We agreed to meet at a park by my parents' house in Forest Hill.

There was a pavilion in the park next to some ballfields, and as I pulled into the empty parking lot I hopped out and walked up to that area. I'll never forget what I was wearing that day because in my smug ego-driven madness, I wanted to show these cops who they were dealing with. I had on a $600 maroon woven Coogi sweater with a big chunky gold chain around my neck, baggy jeans hanging off my ass, and unlaced ox-blood Timberlands. I sat on the picnic table and lit up a cigarette, cocky, waiting on their arrival. When they approached, they had smirks on their faces. I imagined they were thinking, *This kid is the real deal, not someone to play with.* What they were probably actually thinking was, *Who does this goofball think he is?"*

Once introductions were made and they took their seats, I tried to take control of the situation. "Okay, so I was wondering if I was going to ever hear from you guys. Like I was saying months ago at the station, I can show you guys all of the sites where they sell the steroids I was getting—"

I was immediately cut off. "Look, that's great and all, and maybe in the future we'll reach out to you about all of that, but we're going to need some real stuff." He started going in a direction I didn't like and he kept going. "We need to know who's out here with the real drugs, the heroin and the cocaine. Take us to those people, I know you know some old buddies."

I didn't want to take this too abruptly in the wrong direction and leave the pavilion in handcuffs, so instead of flat out telling them *no*, I explained to them that it was impossible for me. "I'm in recovery," I stated proudly. "I don't associate with anyone even remotely close to that lifestyle. I wouldn't even know where to look."

"Bullshit." I was cut off again. "You think we don't know that you're plugged in. You know who's out here doing what. We just need a little help, if you don't want to go to jail. We'll wire you up once or twice…"

I chuckled, "Yeah, okay."

He continued, "Don't worry, it's completely confidential. Nobody knows who our informants are."

I laughed again. "Yeah okay, like Manny? You think I don't know Manny wore a wire on me. You think it's not painfully obvious?"

They both looked at each other, confirming what I just said. "What you think you know..."

I kept going, "I don't think, I know! Manny is the only person I ever dealt with in Baltimore County." Realizing what I just said, I quickly tried to cover up, "Manny is the only person I ever dealt with!"

The Baltimore County detective leaned in close to me, "If I were you, I wouldn't let Manny know you know that. He's hired muscle for a lot of heavy hitters out of East Baltimore, and you know as well as I do that he's probably got bodies on him."

"Fuck Manny. He better hope he don't see me!" I spat back, poking out my chest to prove my bravado to these officers. "I've seen his record, I know him from prison. I know he's got bodies."

I had in fact looked up Manny's record on the Maryland case system. 'Having bodies' meant that he had murders under his belt. I couldn't prove it besides one overdose I knew he was responsible for. However, he had multiple gun cases, robbery, discharging a firearm, drug trafficking, and more spanning the past two decades on his record. The funny thing is that almost every single one of those cases had been 'nolle pros', meaning they didn't follow through with prosecution. It wasn't hard to figure out what was going on.

I continued, "So you've got a dangerous, gun-toting,

cocaine dealer out here feeding you small time white boys selling testosterone and fat burners from the suburbs? How does that make sense to you?" I was on a roll, "Not to mention, half of my clientele worked within your ranks as police and correctional officers. You're worried about me selling workout supplements to regular people in the community instead of him?" That got their attention, and I immediately regretted it.

The Harford County officer spoke up, "So, that's another thing we wanted to speak to you about. Would you be willing to help reveal to us who those people in law enforcement were that you were dealing with?"

"Absolutely not," I replied firmly and immediately. "I'd be better off telling on a drug dealer than the police. So what? I could get pulled over and have drugs planted on me—or worse? No way."

At this point I could tell the Harford County detective was sure this was a waste of his time, and the Baltimore County guy chuckled to himself in frustration. He wrote his cell phone number down on the back of his business card and told me, "I'll give you thirty days to find out who's selling cocaine or heroin and then call me, and we'll go from there. If I don't hear from you, you're going to jail."

I played into his threats, "Yes sir, you'll be hearing from me soon." I slid the card into my pocket. I had no intention of ever calling him, but I knew it would buy me some time. Maybe he would call me in thirty days, and I could bluff him for another month or two. In my mind they were completely out of line. I had explained to them I was a recovering addict, and yet they wanted me to start hanging around drug dealers and making controlled buys of the very drugs I was once addicted to. My life didn't matter to them one bit. I did not plan on cooperating, but this lit an extra fire of anger within me that convinced me to not even entertain them anymore.

That's exactly what I did. I let the situation drift away into a forgotten back corner of my mind. I knew they had exactly a year and a day from the date of my initial arrest to file charges on me. The closer it got to that date, the more I thought I had escaped charges. But then about eleven and a half months after the arrest date, an officer arrived at my door to serve me with a five-count criminal indictment in the Circuit Court of Baltimore County. I was being charged with three counts of distribution of a drug other than marijuana and two counts of possession. The paperwork detailed three meetings between Manny, who was only identified by a number, in different parking lots on route 40 in Baltimore County. I guessed, as the officer had put it, I was going to jail.

I had no choice but to carry on with my usual pointless existence. I had no sense of purpose and no future, so I lived for the daily satisfaction of my ego. I still had my job waiting tables at the restaurant, but by no means was I going back to selling any illegal drugs. I hustled hard at my eBay store, traveling to department stores all over the tri-state area in search of brand name clothing that I could flip for profit. I made a few hundred dollars a week doing this, but it was never enough. My desire for quick money in order to buy material things, which in turn gave me the appearance of having money so I could attract women once again drew out my creativity. Through the deep recesses of the internet I discovered a hook up in New York for diamond watches. I could buy Joe Rodeo and Aquamaster watches for $150 and sell them at the barber shops around town and to guys at the gym for $500-600. These watches were covered in minuscule diamonds, but at the time they were very trendy among the urban crowd. This side gig earned me some extra clout and credibility in the street market, so I started searching for other things to sell.

Soon I found seven-star replicas of Louis Vuitton purses on the internet. I knew I could purchase these purses for $150 apiece and sell them for upwards of $1,000. The replicas came from China, and included everything a regular LV bag would come with: the same hardware, identification code on the inside, cloth bag, box, and even a fake receipt. I justified to myself that if the people buying them thought they were authentic and nobody knew the difference, then I wasn't really ripping anyone off. My ego was in full control and taking me for another ride. I could justify anything I wanted to do in order to satisfy it.

I received my first shipment of purses from China. When I opened the box, I was confused and angry. They had ripped me off! I opened a box full of cheap, generic-looking, leather purses. They were nothing like the perfect Louie Vuitton replicas I had ordered. In fact, they had no brand on them at all; they were junk. Frustrated, I piled them one after the other onto my kitchen counter wondering what I was going to do with them. As I did, something caught my eye.

The seam of one of the purses had started to come apart. I stuck my finger in the hole and began to break it open further and was both shocked and pleased by what I found inside. These masterminds had sewn cheap, fake purses around the Louie Vuitton replicas in order to get past customs or any other kind of search. Within each one of these generic leather bags was a perfect replica LV bag covered with their popular monogram, including the 'authenticity card' and a mock receipt.

I got straight to work selling them on eBay. By the end

of the week, they had all sold between $600 and $900 each. I was eager to make big money now. I placed another order and repeated the process, but I remained nervous that upon arrival any one of my customers would report me for selling fake bags. My reviews were perfect though. People were thanking me for the amazing and authentic bag. I was now confident enough to sell to people who I knew in person. I took them to the restaurant and sold them to the girls there. They went crazy for them.

All good things must come to an end though, especially all good 'bad' things. Only a few weeks into my new enterprise, I was shut down. I got a message from eBay that my store was being temporarily shut down because a representative of Louis Vuitton had reported me for selling fake merchandise. Of course, as a scavenger, I was used to this by now and began looking for my next hustle.

During these months two court dates came and went for the distribution indictment. They had been postponed because the state couldn't get their side together. On the first date, they postponed because they hadn't gotten a chemist who could lab test the steroids, and on the second date, they postponed because they hadn't gotten the lab results back yet. I had lawyered up with the money I made from my eBay store. The lawyer I had hired was the husband of the public defender who had gone to bat for me during my addiction. I felt I at least owed it to them to pay them for anything I needed help with during my days of sobriety.

I navigated life with both trepidation and the risk of someone with nothing left to lose. On one hand, I toed the line because I couldn't risk going back to jail and ruining the little bit of life I had gained clean and sober. On the other hand,

I wasn't sure whether my freedom was going to be snatched away when I finally went to court. So I didn't plan for the future; instead I lived irresponsibly in the moment. I blew every bit of money I had on clothing, and gym supplements, and eating out at restaurants. I still lived in my parents' house, and on nights when I wasn't over at Maria's house, I was on the computer talking nasty with women in chat rooms. One night when she was in the basement of my parents' house helping me take pictures of clothing and list them on my eBay store, I left her alone for several minutes to go outside and smoke a cigarette. When I returned, she was sitting in front of my computer with tears streaming down her face.

A message had pinged on the screen and she read it in disbelief. Then, she scrolled back and read a lot more messages full of sexual flirtation. For years this sort of behavior was an outlet for me, a way to feed my ego, and now I had been caught red handed. I did what every fragile, insecure person does best, I attempted to flip it on her.

"Why are you snooping through my stuff?" I feigned anger at her, and tried in my own narcissistic way to act like it was her fault she found these things. It was my own fragile lie I was trying so hard to protect, and I felt like my life depended on it. I was able to convince myself she was as wrong as I was, now I just had to convince her of the same. In hindsight I was a monster, but at that time I was just a scared animal in a trap.

I was able to do an adequate job of convincing her and myself, and promising her it would never happen again. Within hours I was cradling her against me as she cried. I cried too, telling her how much I loved her and how sorry I was. But lust when used as ego fuel, is like a drug. I knew I couldn't put it down that easily.

LEVEL FOUR

We don't see things as they are, we see things as we are.

—Anais Nin

ACCORDING TO SCIENCE, each cell in our body essentially dies off and replaces itself every seven years. Some cells die off and are reborn in a matter of days, others take years. Either way, in seven years not a single cell that is in my body right now will be here. Physically I will be an entirely new human being. I often use this as evidence of a soul or spirit within us that lives apart from our bodies. If my body is completely new, then how am I still the same me? Also, it is said that the physical universe is a reflection of the spirit, which would explain why our physical appearances continue to age even though the cells that comprise our bodies are constantly being renewed. Further, it is commonly believed that our emotional and spiritual growth is stunted the moment we become dependent on drugs and/ or alcohol. I started drinking and drugging at the age of 14, then stopped at the age of 23. This meant I had the emotional maturity of a 14-year-old when I finally got clean at the age of 23. My body reflected that as well; I always looked young for my age.

By age 28 I had been clean for over five years, but I had done nothing to address my emotional immaturity other than fill the void with every distraction I could. I sat in meetings for years, but never worked the twelve steps. I read books and went to church, but never applied any of the principles I learned to my life. Instead, I chased my ego down a dark, lonely road of immaturity and stunted growth, pursuing lust, power, importance, greed, and every other temptation life threw at me. They all left me just as lonely and broken as when I started.

The world continued revolving without me. My peers outgrew me. People came and went, and yet I was still a scared little boy with big muscles and a big gold chain living in Mommy and Daddy's house. I was 28 years old going on 18 and still wanted to fight every guy who looked at me wrong and sleep with every girl I came across because that's what I thought mattered. I thought somehow if I could be the toughest, most desirable man in the room, it would bury the fact that I was actually a loser who was terrified of responsibility.

Maria had saved up enough money by now to get out of her mother's house and buy an apartment of her own and move closer to the city. She was a few years younger than me and yet way ahead of me in maturity. We had been together for almost five years at this point, and it would have made sense to finally move out of my parents' house and into her apartment to split the bills with her. I was too much of a coward. I was terrified of the responsibility and the commitment. These were two things I had never embraced in life. Rather I had intentionally dodged repeatedly.

I drove forty minutes to her apartment every night and then forty minutes home, no matter how late it was. I could've stayed there, but the sense of commitment and finality of it all scared me. I would come up with excuses of course, rather than admit any of it to myself or anyone else. She struggled waitressing on weekends and working a 9-5 job to pay for her apartment and all of her bills. I was there every night, and we had two cats who lived there as well, yet I never contributed a dollar to help her out. When I did stay the night, I would sleep on the couch while she slept in the bedroom. She would wake up early in the morning for work and come over and kiss me on her way out as I lay sleeping on her couch. I would sleep in as long as I wanted, then leave to go play around shopping for the eBay store or meet up with other women.

Looking back, I'm ashamed and heartbroken by my behavior, but at the time my toxic ego told me she was lucky to have a guy like me. It didn't help that most of the guys I spoke with were stuck in the same mental rut as I was, so it was easily justifiable because they were doing the same things. We were not men; we were cowards who had a misconception of what a man really was. And it would become one of the last lessons I'd learn. We prided ourselves on how much money we could get women to spend on us, rather than what we were willing to spend on them. We would brag about how many women we could sleep with and how much we could get away with. Deep down inside, there was a loving little boy, but I had found new walls to protect him. Of course, these walls were toxic and destructive, just like drugs and alcohol.

I watched Maria struggle and suffer, and all I had to offer her was sex and some occasional comforting words. If I gave her $50 or cleaned her apartment while she was at work, I would make a huge deal out of it. I looked at it as a gift, instead of the duty that it actually was. She stayed with me out of her own insecurities. I was aware of this, and it kept me secure in the relationship. However, she was outgrowing me, and I felt it. She had a professional day job, and now a place of her own. I was still waiting tables and living in my parents' house. I knew the day would come when she would wake up and say enough is enough.

Court came. My lawyer tried to convince me to cooperate with the detectives and out a few drug dealers. "We can postpone it one more time. You can just give them what they want and walk away from it all."

I snapped at him, "This is not what I hired you for!"

"You've been watching those 'Stop Snitching' videos, haven't you?" he remarked, half joking, in reference to recent videos that had arisen out of Baltimore about killing snitches.

That wasn't the case at all. It wasn't about not snitching out of fear for repercussions; I never even got that far down that line of thinking. Even though I may have been a coward when it came to women, there were some things I found strength in standing behind. One of them was the principle of personal responsibility. I believed if I did something wrong and got caught, then it was my responsibility to own the repercussions like a man. At no point, could I get caught doing something wrong and then tell on someone else in order to weasel my way out of it. That is not what a man does; that is what a coward does. I could never make someone else pay for the mistakes I made. I had to own them, and at some point, they would own their own. This was my line of thinking. If somebody did something horrible and I got blamed for it, then it might have been a different story, I wasn't prepared to lose years of my life for someone else's wrongdoings, just like I wasn't prepared to make someone lose years of their life for mine. One of the principles I prided my recovery on is personal responsibility, so in this issue I took a hard stand.

We entered the courtroom in Towson Circuit courthouse and took a seat. I sat and listened as a Mexican woman was brought before the judge. She needed a translator, and she stood horrified shaking in her shackles as I listened to the details of her case. She was in the country illegally and had been driving down Towson Town Blvd when a lady pushing a baby in a stroller had crossed the roadway. She accidentally plowed into the stroller killing the baby instantly. Panicking, and not knowing what to do, she drove another couple hundred feet before pulling over. She then got out and retrieved the mangled baby and stroller from where it had been wedged between her tire and the wheel well, grinding horrifically against the tread. She discarded them there on the median and hopped back into her truck and sped off.

As horrific as her actions had been, my heart broke for her. I was obviously also heartbroken for the woman who lost her baby in such a disgusting manner and had to witness this tragedy. I couldn't even imagine the level of pain she was going through. However, I also put myself in the shoes of the woman in front of me. She's in a new country surrounded by strangers who don't speak her language. She's just caused a horrible accident that I'm sure she feels extremely guilty for. She knows she doesn't belong here, has no way to communicate with the victims, and probably expects to be torn apart for what she just did. So she sped off, and as wrong as it was, I didn't blame her. I sat there horrified and wanting to cry, and it wasn't even my trial. I was questioning God and the evils of this world as I sat there forgetting I was there for my own petty issues.

When my name was called, I was ready for whatever was going to happen. I was expecting another postponement. The case had been dragged out for over two years over a simple steroid possession. I knew there was no way they were going to blow Manny's cover as an informant by bringing him on the stand because they had him working on much bigger fish in the cocaine industry. I also knew they weren't equipped to deal with steroid cases. In fact, I may have been their first one in a multitude of years since they couldn't even find a chemist or lab to test what I was caught with. All of these factors gave me confidence walking into trial, and I was correct to feel that way. My lawyer approached the stand and came back a few minutes later.

"They're dropping the distribution charge and just charging you with possession. We'll get you a probation before judgement, and you'll just have to do like 25 hours of community service to make them happy. Sound good to you?"

"Let's go" I replied, letting out a deep sigh of relief. This is what I'd hoped for. No more stress, no more waiting and looking over my shoulder. This also meant no more excuses. It was time to do something with my life.

My attorney nodded to the judge and state attorney, and just like that, the judge repeated aloud the same thing my lawyer had just whispered to me. I was walking out of the courtroom a free man. Even though I believed the state was making a mountain out of a mole hill, the fact remained that I had broken the law, got caught, and things could have gone much worse. I thanked God, but I had thanked God often. When was I going to start living like I was grateful?

I always had an acute talent for missing the boat. I would toy with an idea over and over so that by the time I had made a decision it was too late. I missed the mark big time in the mortgage industry. My father had given up real estate for a while as the industry had slowed down, and he got a job working for a subprime mortgage broker. This was in the height of the mortgage boom, and he was doing better than he ever had before. I started doing clerical work and credit checks for him on the side for a little while and began familiarizing myself with the business. Once the court date for steroids was over, I figured it was time to really make a shift in my life and take a chance. I asked him to plug me in with some loan officers he dealt with and see if any of them would hire me.

He gave me leads with three different local firms in which the managers said they could get me a job as a mortgage broker, even with my criminal record. I interviewed with the first two, and they offered me the jobs. But upon receiving my record back from the state, they had to inform me they couldn't hire me. I had four pages of criminal charges on my record relating to my previous addiction, but the one that came back to haunt me and would continue to haunt me for the rest of my life was my very first charge as an adult. The charge of forgery and fraudulent check writing from when I stole my parents checks at age 18 and wrote them out to myself would prove to be a thorn in my side for the next twenty years. In my mind it was the least of all the evils I had committed in my active addiction, but to an employer who would be placing me in a fiduciary position of trust, it was the worst.

I walked into the third mortgage brokers office pretty much defeated, but trying my luck, and was hired on the spot. It was the closest to my house, only a couple miles away on Main St. in the small town of Bel Air. The office took up the whole first floor of a giant white Victorian house situated between the county office building and a law firm. This was a new step for me. I always dreamed of being in the professional world and having an actual career. Now I could dress up, eat lunch on Main St with other professionals, and work with other business people. I expected a new world to unfold before me. It was anything but that.

I entered the mortgage industry right as it was collapsing in 2008. Of course, I didn't know that at the time. I was given a basic script to deliver over the telephone. Two other guys and I shared an open area in the front of the office where we were handed lists of leads. The lists consisted of thousands of phone numbers, most of which did not work. We were to cold call these people all day long to try to get anyone who would possibly bite on the idea of a refinance. This job was the exact opposite of what I was prepared for or qualified for. I was a shy introvert, the complete opposite of a pushy salesperson. I could not convince people to purchase products that were not going to benefit them or that they were not interested in. Because of my morals and integrity when it came to other people's finances and well-being, I knew there was no chance of me striking it rich in this industry like I had learned so many others had done. The two owners of my branch could tell anyone anything they wanted to hear, no matter how big of a deception it was. That wasn't for me. I just couldn't do it.

Still, day after day I plugged away at the lists, often times getting cursed out or led along on a practical joke by the rare few who actually answered our cold calls. I watched the owners scream daily at other employees and at each other. They never directed it towards me, and I think it's because they knew I wouldn't take that kind of treatment. They often called me the "thug," "criminal," or "Coogi" in jest because of the big colorful Coogi sweaters I wore on casual days. Every day was a daily scream fest in our office, as I spoke low to potential customers on the telephone while they screamed at an employee behind me or called them 'faggots' and talked about 'banging their girlfriends.' It was more like a college dorm than a professional office setting. One owner and a couple of the senior guys in our office spent their whole days bouncing between online poker and world of warcraft.

Somehow in the insanity, I manage to secure a couple of legit refinances over the phone with people in other states who could really benefit from them. I also did a couple refinances for friends and a purchase loan for my brother. Within a couple months most of the loan officers had come and gone, and I became the top producer in the office with just my few deals. This quickly earned me my own office, as the previous top producer relapsed on alcohol and stopped showing up for work most days. By the time I averaged out the commissions versus the time I spent in the office, I was only earning slightly above minimum wage. Yet, having my own office made me feel extremely important and gave my life whole new meaning.

Having my own office also meant that my activity on the computer would no longer be closely monitored by the office owners looking over my shoulder. I conveniently positioned my desk to face the door so my screen wasn't visible to anyone entering my office. It didn't take long before I delved into the world of online poker with the other members of the office. My actual work took a backseat, and simultaneously the stress in the office grew. The leads were getting worse, and no loans were being closed by anyone.

Online poker became my new addiction. I convinced the owner that I needed to stay late for work on a few occasions, and he entrusted me with a key to the office. This was a huge step for me. I felt like a real-life responsible businessman. Me, a junkie who couldn't be trusted in my own parents' house alone years before, who had stolen anything that wasn't nailed down, was just given the keys to an entire office building. The ultimate irony in all of it was that I couldn't see I was still violating this new trust for devious purposes. I wasn't staying late for work. I was staying in the office until the wee hours of the morning playing poker on the internet.

I didn't have a lot of money, so I would only play tournaments that would cost between five and twenty dollars to buy into. However, these tournaments would have several hundred players, so depending on how long I lasted, sometimes the games carried on for six to eight hours. Playing for hours at a time and making it to the final tables was an adrenaline rush. I would often play well enough for several hours and get right to the point where I was about to win money, then my anxiety would get the best of me, and I would make rash decisions and lose right before the miracle happened. I quickly learned that the game of Texas Hold 'Em mirrors real life. The intensity made the game all that more addictive.

In the game of Texas Hold 'Em, you get dealt two cards face down that are only yours, then three cards are flopped, which become the community cards. You must make the most out of your hold cards in conjunction with the three community cards and determine how valuable your hand is. After a round of betting, another community card is flopped, then another round of betting, and then a final community card. At this point, between your two personal cards and the five public cards you must determine your best hand and its value, if you haven't already folded to previous betting.

In his song *The Gambler*, Kenny Rogers sings, "You gotta know when to hold 'em, and when to fold 'em" in reference to the game of life. We are all dealt our own cards, whether in life as a whole, yearly, monthly, or daily. It is up to us to play those cards wisely. Maybe you get dealt good hold cards, and you're born into wealth and a loving family, but the flop is tragic for you. Maybe the flop is perfect for you, and you play your cards wrong and make bad decisions with drugs, drinking, relationships, etc. Or maybe you get dealt bad cards, but you play them wisely and carefully and make the most out of them. Maybe you bluff your way through several hands while holding bad cards and make something out of nothing. The point is that in every way, the game of Texas Hold 'Em poker mirrors real life in its entirety. There are times where another player in your life may call you all in, and you must make the decision to stand or back down, and if you have the strength and repose to stand behind that decision it may work out favorably for you. Sometimes you must be patient and fold repeatedly, every day, until you have a hand to play. Other times you must finally decide life isn't dealing you the hands you want, and if you don't make a decision quickly to take action, then you are going to run out of time and money.

It was an adrenaline rush, no matter that there was only a little bit of money on the line. As long as there was just enough money to make people play semi-serious then I found it highly enjoyable and addicting. The problem, like everything else I ever found addicting, is that it became my primary focus and everything else in my life took a back burner. Staying in the office by myself until two to four in the morning also gave me another devious idea. I could use the office to invite women over. I was still dating Maria, but that never stopped me before. I started chatting up women online and spent all of my time bouncing back and forth between the chatrooms and poker rooms.

As tension grew in the office, and tempers roared over the failing business, I laid low and kept to myself. Multiple employees were fired, and eventually the partners split. Because I laid low,

I was given pats on the back. I knew the remaining owner was treading lightly to keep one of his only remaining employees. As far as he knew, I was hard at work in my office trying to close loans. Instead, I was doing everything but that. I was resenting the position I was given calling and harassing lists of cold leads and the way my boss swindled customers out of money with lies and manipulation. My revenge, I reasoned, was wasting his time by sitting in the office all day getting paid to do whatever I wanted, then inviting various women into the office at night.

On several occasions I had strange women from the chatrooms on the internet come to the office after all of the employees had left. We'd have sex, role-play in my office, or sometimes for an extra thrill, we'd have sex on the boss' desk. The ultimate irony of finally getting a professional job and a key to the office was what I chose to do with it. I was clearly far from ready, and way too immature, to handle any semblance of responsibility.

I had garnered a decent amount of speeding tickets during my daily travels and had to turn my license in to the local MVA for a 30-day suspension. Once my license was turned in my 30-day suspension automatically began. The idea, I suppose, was to have someone drive me to the MVA to drop off my license so I wasn't therefore driving home on a suspended license. That was too complicated for me; I chose to do it the easy way. Certain no one would notice, I dropped my license off, then drove from the MVA straight to work. My plan was to stay at work late, then drive the five miles or so home, under the cover of night. It was Halloween night, my birthday, and the police would be way too busy with other calls to pay attention to me driving home carefully… or so I thought.

Around 1 AM I locked up the office and walked to my car. I was parked alone in a state office building parking lot. It was quiet there, but just a block up the street I could hear the music and yelling coming from all the bars that littered Main St, Bel Air. I got into my car, and pulled out of the empty parking lot onto Main St, and drove about 10 feet before I heard the whirl of a siren and the blinding red and blue lights in my rearview. *How is this possible?* I was dumbfounded, I hadn't driven more than 20 feet. I pulled over to the curb as the police vehicle pulled in behind me and sat there for a few minutes watching drunken young people stagger down sidewalks, some propping each other up. A guy and a girl screamed at each other on the other side of the street, and a drunk stumbled across the intersection in front of me. There were hundreds of partygoers everywhere. Why was this cop wasting his time with me?

As he approached my car, I could see that he was very young, maybe nineteen years old and of Asian descent. He ordered me to hand over my license and registration in an angry voice.

"Can I ask why you're pulling me over? I didn't do anything wrong," I stated.

He jumped back suddenly as if I had challenged him to a fight. Standing about five feet away from my car window, he danced around in the street, "Do you have a fucking problem? Huh? Do you have a fucking problem with me?"

I was shocked and in disbelief. Did he know me and have a previous issue with me? I could swear I'd never seen him before. I rolled my eyes at his ridiculous display. "Whoa, calm down tough guy, nobody's got a problem. I was just curious why you pulled me over when there's clearly more serious things going on."

As if on cue, a pickup truck full of drunken young people in Halloween masks drove by yelling and screaming. One of them hollered, "You fucking pig!!" It was like an exclamation point at the end of my sentence. I half expected him to leave me alone and pursue them, but he was unphased.

Throughout our encounter, several more drunk people shouted at him and called him names. One girl yelled his way, "Why can't you assholes leave people alone?" I silently wished just one of them would distract him from me, but no such luck.

He came back to my vehicle abruptly. "Sir, I'm going to need you to step out of the vehicle, now!" My heart dropped. "Do it slowly! Both hands where I can see them!"

I complied. He pushed me against the car, wrenched my arms behind my back and cuffed me.

"What did I do? What is this about?" I repeatedly asked him and received no answer in return. My mind raced. Had I been falsely identified in a robbery? Was there something from my past that had come back to haunt me? Did I rob him, hurt, or steal from him during my addiction and now he is getting revenge? Without a word I was stuffed into the back of the squad car as the circus of drunken insanity whirred around us on Main St.

Once at the station, he explained that he had arrested me for driving on a suspended license. I was blown away that he had not only arrested me, but treated me so harshly for this. I told him about my history of crime and addiction, and he told me he was new on the force in Bel Air, that he had just transferred from Baltimore City. After discussing some of the streets and neighborhoods I had run around in and survived, he almost developed a kind of respect for me and began treating me kindly. It didn't prevent him from taking me to jail though.

Several years clean, I was taken back to the Harford County Detention Center. I heard the familiar click of the gate as it closed behind me and smelled the old, depressing scent of the state soap that is ingrained into the very foundation of that place. I sat shackled on a wooden bench for a few hours before a commissioner was able to see me. They placed me on a one thousand dollar bail, with 10% cash acceptable. I paid the $100 on a credit card, and they unshackled me. Then I was allowed to call my mother for a ride home. It was 6:30 in the morning, and I felt empty inside calling my mother for a ride home from jail yet again, and yet I had a sense of pride that I was actually able to pay my own bail.

I went to court thirty days later, and the judge sentenced me sixty days in jail. Sixty days for my first time ever to drive on a suspended license. Because of my extensive history involving the law, I was given the maximum. I took at as a small price to pay for all the things I had done in the past. Rather than dwelling in pity like I easily might have, I chose to take it on the chin and keep moving forward. The events leading up to it seemed like a bad dream. It was strangely unfair, if I chose to look at it that way: the fact that I got pulled over after driving only twenty feet, only hours after getting my license suspended, and then the way I was treated by the officer. I was taken to jail unnecessarily, and given a bail unnecessarily, and then handed the maximum sentence in court. I could have easily justified using this situation to backslide, or fall into depression, or at least throw a massive pity party. However, if I had learned anything in my recovery, it was to stand tall, be proud, and change my perception. After all, I didn't make the best decisions early on. In fact, I frequently made horrible decisions in my day-to-day life, but when it came to adversity, I knew that my fate depended upon how I handled it. This time, I handled it like a boss. I was proud to pay for my misdeeds. I absolutely did not want to go back to jail, but I realized I had no choice, and so the only way to do it was proudly with my chest out and get it over with.

The judge respected the fact that I had a steady employer and gave me the opportunity to do my time on work release. He also gave me two weeks to set it up and then turn myself in. This was the first time I had ever been given this kind of opportunity. I was used to being handcuffed in the courtroom and carted off to jail, but then again, I had never held a steady job in my previous life of crime. I was sure my boss at the mortgage company was not going to come sign me out on work release, so I was prepared to return to Bertucci's and see if they would do it for me. However, to my surprise, when I asked my current employer, he obliged and went to the jail to sign me out.

I turned myself in shortly after and went through the all too familiar and humiliating routine of booking at the detention center. I was stripped naked, made to expose every crack and crevice of my body to the onlooking officer, take a cold shower with lice soap, and then put on my black and white stripes. They sent me off to a low-security tier awaiting my work release. It usually takes a couple days to be completely registered and verified for work release and then be moved downstairs to an actual work release unit. I bided my time as if I was on a mini-vacation, reading Dan Brown novels and dining on fine jail cuisine. *This is nothing. I'll be back outside working in two or three days,* I thought.

After three days of not hearing my name called, I began to

get paranoid. I began asking questions to every officer I came across and submitting slips to the work release unit. Day after day nobody responded. I called Maria, no answer. I mailed her letters every night, and eagerly awaited mail call. Every night came and went with no letters and no replies from work release. My father was a busy man, but I was frantic. *Why am I stuck in jail?* I had him start looking into things. After days of research and phone calls, it turned out that I had a warrant in Baltimore City for a trespassing charge from 2006, and that is why the work release unit wouldn't take me. I had never gotten a trespassing charge in the city during my years of sobriety! I tried to explain this to everyone, but nobody believed me. *How is this possible?* I was losing my mind in jail. This little 60-day sentence had turned into a full-blown nightmare. I had been in jail for four full weeks. Maria disappeared the second I went in. And now I was being unfairly held for something I didn't do.

It turned out that the charge in the city had a one-thousand-dollar bail on the warrant. If my father paid the bail, then he would get the money back when I went to court, and work release would accept me. On his day off, he paid the bail for me, and a few days later I was finally taken down to the work release unit. I barely slept that night in anticipation of being in the outside world again and finding out why Maria wasn't answering or writing to me. I loved her. She had stuck by me through everything. I had finally come to realize how amazing she was and that I had a lot of growing up to do, and there was no better time than now to start. I thought long and hard in jail about my future and how much I missed and adored her. I was ready to commit fully to her and stop the childish games with other women. I had done enough damage to Maria, and she didn't deserve any of it. She was perfect to me.

I was also going to quit smoking. This four weeks in jail without a cigarette had given me enough of a reprieve and time to think about improving my life that for the first time ever, I decided not to smoke upon release. The next morning, I finally stepped out into the world and happily headed to the mortgage office, not knowing what layed in wait.

I arrived back at the office for the first day in weeks ready to try to sink back into my work and get focused on sales. I turned on my computer and there was an email from Maria. It began, "Dan, I know you will be getting out on work release any day now..." It went on to say she was done, and that it was over. There wasn't much of an explanation, just that it was something she had to do. This chapter in her life was over, and she had finally found an opportunity to close the door. She asked me not to contact her and make things harder than they already were. She said she was crying and broken inside, that it had crushed her to do this, but it was what she had to do.

As I read her words, tears streamed down my face. I hurt. My whole heart ached as I sat in front of the computer, frozen. Five years with Maria had come to a full halt, and I knew there was no saving it. I could sense things were truly over, and there was no salvaging it. Her words held such a sense of finality and a feeling of pain. I knew if I was any sort of man, then I had to leave her be. I knew I deserved the worst because of what I had done throughout our relationship. I could justify my actions when I spoke to other people by saying, "I warned her I wasn't relationship material when we got together." And, "She knew what type of guy I was." Or, "I told her repeatedly that I wasn't ready to settle down." I used these and many other justifications to help ease myself of the blame. While all of these statements were true, we did grow close after one night of casual sex. And while I did in fact make it known that I would sleep with other women and wasn't ready to settle down, the reality is that I strung her along for years and wasted an important chunk of her life. It was unfair to her. In my moments of weakness, I clung to her for support and professed my love to her. Then in my moments of strength, I cast her to the side and chased ego-fulfillment in other women. I knew I deserved to be left alone.

I made one half-assed attempt to contact her, and she replied by sending me a music video to a popular song at the time. She said the song spoke perfectly about how she felt. I hadn't heard it, but as I opened the video and listened to *Big Girls Don't Cry* by Fergie, I cried like a baby. As she sung the beautiful lyrics "I hope you know, I hope you know that this has nothing to do with you. It's personal, myself and I. We've got some straightening out to do. And I'm gonna miss you like a child misses their blanket. But I've got to get a move on with my life. It's time to be a big girl now, and big girls don't cry." I sobbed at my computer. For a couple of days, I watched the video and wallowed in my grief and cried over my newfound loss. There was one thing that puzzled me about the lyrics, the fact that she said they described her situation perfectly. "This has nothing to do with you, its personal..." What did that mean? I would soon find out.

Every event in our lives can be taken as a lesson and used as a tool for growth, especially if these events were caused by our own poor decisions. I had taken Maria for granted. The more she loved me, the more I pulled away. In retrospect, I didn't love myself or feel that I deserved to be loved. This meant that her love would never be good enough for me, so I sought constant validation from other women. *One woman could definitely be wrong about me, but if many were willing to have sex with me, well then, I am lovable, right?*

I damaged Maria early on, then kept at it for years. She loved me unconditionally and kept on loving me and supporting me in my hardest times. When my heart finally began to unfold to her, when I finally realized what I had, it was too late. The damage was already done, and it was irreversible. Even if we had tried to salvage the relationship, the trust could never be regained, and there would always be resentment.

I completed my remaining thirty days on work release as a lifeless, empty shell. I was sad and depressed all day at the office, then returned to jail at night with no intention of making friends with the other inmates. There was a guy in the work release dorm with me who I had grown up with, but I barely exchanged words with him. He was serving a year-long sentence, but was not work release eligible. Instead, he worked at the landfill for a dollar a day to knock time off of his sentence. When I would come back from work release in the evenings, he and another guy would appear to be high on heroin. They would nod out sitting up and drool all over themselves and fall over on their bunks. I finally asked someone how they were managing to get heroin in the jail, and they explained to me that it wasn't heroin; it was a new drug called Suboxone that opiate addicts were given for withdrawal or as a blocker. The active chemical in Suboxone is buprenorphine, which they call 'bupe' on the streets. Addicts would 'toot a bupe,' which meant crushing the Suboxone up and sniffing it for a faster, stronger effect. I was disgusted and wanted nothing to do with it.

One evening, a guy comes over to me, "Dan? You're Dan McGhee, right?"

"Yeah, what's up? Do I know you from somewhere?"

He smiles wide, "You don't remember me? Bro, I saved your life! My name's John. Remember me now? I'm the guy who found you!?"

I wanted to hide. I definitely didn't feel like dealing with this guy in here. He had approached me at a house party years ago with the same excitement and not-so-formal introduction. I remembered from our last encounter that he was one of the two guys who had been walking to work early one March morning, almost ten years prior, and had found my body lying on some church steps in Bel Air. I had been left for dead after an overdose, and had suffered a heart attack and hypothermia. He had called the police to report a dead body, and I was brought back to life at the local hospital.

When he had run into me at a house party shortly after, he introduced himself in the same manner, as "John, the guy who saved your life," smiling through a big, devious grin. At that time, he lectured me about heroin and how horrible it was, and how "no one likes a junkie." Now, here he was re-introducing himself to me at the Harford County Detention Center, and I quickly learned that he was in there due to repercussions from his own heroin addiction he had formed in the previous few years. It seemed to be taking everyone, especially the unsuspecting.

I completed work release and returned home to live at my parents' house again. The mortgage industry had been rocked with some news that was going to severely impact my future. In light of all of the insanity transpiring in unregulated subprime lending, a law was being passed that would require all mortgage professionals to obtain a state license. After some research, I quickly learned that I was not a candidate for licensure due to my criminal record. I didn't fight it; I knew it was time to move on anyway. My experience in the industry had been much less than savory, and I honestly made three times as much money waiting tables. I knew that Bertucci's would gladly take me back.

I contacted the management at Bertucci's and went back to work part-time while I waited for the hammer to drop at the mortgage company and for them to let me go for good. It didn't take long, and when the news came, I didn't take it hard at all. I knew it was coming. It was the story of my life—my criminal history would continue to haunt me forever. Never mind that it had been a decade since those crimes were committed, and forget the fact that they were committed by a reckless teenager. America is unforgiving. Still, I had no one to blame but myself. It just meant that if I wanted to succeed in this world, I'd have to do it creatively.

I had only been home from jail for a little over a month when during idle conversation at Bertucci's, one of the waitresses who had been mutual friends with Maria and I mentioned casually in conversation, "…and you know, I haven't seen Maria since she got pregnant."

"Wait. What did you just say?" I stopped her dead in her tracks.

"Maria is pregnant. I thought you knew."

"Did you hear this from her or have you seen it for yourself?" I snapped.

"No," she said quietly, searching for a way out of our conversation, "but everybody's been talking about it."

My mind was reeling in a thousand different directions. I called a couple of people who I thought could answer me, but no one picked up the phone. I dismissed it as a lie at first, but maybe this was the reason for the abrupt breakup. *Maybe she wants to keep my child from me. I mean, it definitely could be mine, right?* I mused to myself. I even called my parents. I called everybody. *Is this some big trick being played on me that everyone is in on? Is she having my baby, and I am such a loser that everyone thinks it best to keep it a secret from me?*

I got home that night and called Maria's best friend, who I never spoke to. She answered. "Dan, listen, I can't say a whole lot because it's not up to me to do so. But I can tell you that it's not yours. Maria needs to man up and tell you herself. Call her tomorrow. I'll tell her to accept your call and to talk to you."

I was in denial. *She isn't really pregnant, and if she is, then it has to be mine. There is no way it could be someone else's,* I thought to myself while going over the timeline in my head. The next day I bought a pack of cigarettes. I walked into my driveway and dialed Maria's number.

"Hello Dan," her sweet voice came through the receiver as if ready to soothe me before delivering a fatal strike.

"Is it true?" I blurted out. It was the first sentence I'd spoken to her in over a month.

"Yes, it's true. It happened on a weekend when you weren't around. Ty, my ex, kept trying to get back together with me and promising me the world. You and I had been falling to pieces for so long it seemed, that I decided to try it with him, just one night and see if I felt anything, you know.... see if there was something there."

"And you couldn't do that without fucking?" I replied, in the back of my mind knowing I deserved all of this.

She kept going, "I didn't intend on getting pregnant. I didn't want to. You know I'm on birth control, and we used protection. I don't play that shit. But it just happened—"

I cut her off again, "So, you had sex one time with a condom and birth control, and you got pregnant, and I'm supposed to believe that it's not mine?"

"I don't know what to tell you, Dan, it is what it is. I didn't want this to happen. I don't want to be with him, but this is how it happened, and you know my story with abortion. I'll never do it again. We've agreed to try to make it work, and he swears he'll be a good father and partner."

I almost made the comment that I would be the same, but I bit my tongue. At that moment, I felt like I was ready to make any sacrifice to have Maria back, even if it meant taking care of someone else's child. I still had some disbelief in her story, but I knew the only real way to find out was to wait until the child was born and see what color it was. Ty and I were on complete opposite ends of the color spectrum.

I had to let her go, though. There was no arguing, rather there was a mutual sadness between us. Her voice and cadence were firm. I knew she thought long and hard about this, and for me to try to change her mind would only further her pain.

"I wish you the best, Maria. I'm here if there's anything I can ever do. I love you and always will." My voice broke on the last few words, and I quickly hung up the phone. I collapsed against the garage door in the summer sun and balled myself up sobbing hysterically. *What have I done?* I never liked finality, and I knew this was it. That door had just shut forever, and I had let go of a good thing.

Deep in that pain, I matured. From that day forward, I never cheated in another relationship. By not cheating, I learned that living right also gave me power. There is a loss of power that occurs when you are living without a moral compass, and you start to understand you deserve the negative consequences that happen to you. When you have a good, faithful partner, but you are not the same, then they have power over you. The power of righteousness far exceeds the illusion of power created by sin and deviousness. I never wanted to live looking over my shoulder, to be under the control of my mistakes, and mostly I never wanted to hurt anyone so deeply again.

The old, immature me would have been mad at Maria. I would have ignored the fact that I had done her wrong so many times. I would have dwelled on the fact that she cheated on me. I would have told the world about her misdeeds and used it to garner pity and emotional support. Instead, I was silent. All I wanted was her happiness. This, I knew she deserved, and I couldn't give it to her.

I acted out. It's the way I medicated my pain—with other women. I was wild and free now, so I acted like it. Myspace had just gained popularity on the internet and gave me access to women all over Baltimore and its suburbs. I began dating and having flings with various women from all different areas. I quickly forgot the situation with Maria, and even though the sting was still there underneath my new facade, I convinced myself I was better off without her. I was almost thirty years old with no future. I was back to waiting tables fulltime and still living at my parents'. The only real achievement I had was my sobriety, and I held onto it tightly. It had been many years since my last drink or drug. I chased all of my problems away by shifting my focus to chasing women.

Life was in the chase. As long as I was chasing after an unattainable happiness, then I didn't have to focus on the sorrow welling up within or the imminent fear of my destitute future. There was nothing there when I looked forward in time, and that terrified me. So I lived life like a child chasing after moments of immediate satisfaction.

From meeting women online in different suburbs around Baltimore, my network grew. I was hanging in nightclubs and dating strippers and putting myself in risky situations, but the urge to use was not there. Instead, I was so caught up in constructing an alpha image of myself that there was no room for drugs and alcohol. I worried about my appearance, and my appeal to women, and being popular. I often glorified my days selling drugs, yet rarely mentioned my actual drug use and addiction. Meetings and recovery fell to the wayside, and I became a toxic soup of sex addiction and ego centrism.

A guy who owned a recording studio in my barber shop also sold bootleg music CDs, and I would chat him up and buy a couple every week when I was there. One day he handed me a flyer and told me he was hosting a weekly Wednesday night party at a nightclub in Baltimore County. This piqued my interest big time. I wondered how I could get involved in something like that. It could fuel my ego by giving me a small taste of importance. It could give me a purpose to be in the clubs without drinking. And it would put me around tons of beautiful women. I went out that Wednesday to check out his party and support him.

When I arrived the club, he was in the lobby with a couple guys from the barber shop. I handed him five dollars for the cover charge, got my hand stamped, and went inside. It was depressingly empty. There was a huge circular bar surrounded by booths and high-top tables in one room, and in the other room was a dance floor. The DJ was in a tower between the two rooms. Lights danced across the dark empty dance floor while the voices of the bartenders and a few patrons blended into the thumping music. Out of the ten or so people in the strange crowd, I guessed that maybe only half were there because of him. I knew none of them. There were no attractive single women there either, so I walked back out into the lobby and chatted with him for a few minutes.

"This place is awesome, bro," I said encouragingly to him. "We can make this work; I've got a plan. I'll come into the shop and talk to you this week. Give me the opportunity and we can definitely make this happen."

He didn't know me well enough to trust me or not, but I sensed from the complete lack of clientele there, he had to be willing to try anything. *This might be my one chance at a future. I have to land this gig.* I thought maybe, just maybe, I could start a new adventure and build a future for myself making money in the very places that had once been my downfall. After all, these bars and nightclubs owed me for my loyalty to them for so many years ago and for starting me on the spiral that almost killed me. Didn't they?

LEVEL FIVE

Just cause you got the monkey
off your back,
doesn't mean the circus
has left town.

—George Carlin

SOMETIMES THINGS COME into our lives and don't make sense at that very moment. Sometimes these things are meant to be bad for us and our future. But in retrospect, I've learned that everything happens for a reason. In hindsight, our worst decisions can appear to have been divinely inspired. Sometimes we must move backwards a few steps in order to regain our footing and reroute our path. This is exactly what happened when I began promoting nightclub parties. I had no business, as a clean and sober recovering addict and alcoholic, being in a bar or nightclub, let alone hosting parties in them. It was a horrible idea and an absolutely awful gamble with my own life, and yet somehow it worked for me at the time. I was desperate and scrambling to find a way to make a living and build a future. I was also, as always, looking for a way to fulfill my monstrous ego. This was a way to solve both issues at once. Promoting parties would not only give me an income, but it would grant me the importance and attention I'd craved since my childhood.

I met with Mark and convinced him I could definitely get a crowd to the club. We agreed that I would promote the upcoming Wednesday night parties with him and split the cover charge at the end of the night. He had an arrangement with the owner that he would charge a $5 cover at the door, and at the end of the night he would pay the DJ and half of the security team. Any money left after that would be our profit to share. In turn, the owner gave him cheap drink specials to promote and free reign to host any kind of party he wanted. I grabbed a few hundred flyers from Mark with the details of the parties and quickly got to work.

Luckily, I had a vast network to tap into for such a thing as this. I worked in the restaurant industry, and industry people love to drink and party. I also had a huge network of people from my past life of partying and selling drugs. Lastly, and what ended up to be the key factor in getting the initial party started, I was seeing a handful of women from various suburbs of Baltimore City.

I littered the restaurant where I worked with flyers and drove around placing them in stores and handing them out in the streets. I contacted my acquaintances, old and new, and gave them details for the upcoming Wednesday night party, and I urged them to come out. Most of them were confused and wanted to know if I was back to drinking again. "Hell no," I would reply proudly, "I'm just hosting the parties. This is business." I had to walk a fine line between convincing people to come out for fun and not because they were supporting my new means of income. I quickly found out, as I would in most of life's ventures, that the majority of support would come from strangers.

Lastly, I contacted the females I was seeing or had been seeing recently and convinced them to come out to the Wednesday night party and bring all of their friends. I wasn't concerned about them meeting or talking to one another. I wasn't concerned with losing any of the small relationships I'd forged with any of them. This was about the big picture for me. It was about my future.

When Wednesday night finally rolled around, I met Mark at the front door. We set up a table at the entrance with a cash box, plenty of $5 bills for change, an ink stamper to stamp hands, and a clicker to count how many people we brought in. My heart beat out of my chest, and my nerves were raw. This opportunity wasn't just about garnering an income for me, it was a measure of how much I really mattered to people, of how important I really was. It would either bolster my ego or shatter it into a million pieces. I stood at the front door almost physically sick with anxiety as an hour went by and no one arrived.

Then, just before 9:30 people began to trickle in. A few friends came in, followed by a few strangers, and then the girls I had invited arrived with their friends in tow. Shortly, there were several groups of girls sitting around in various places throughout the bar, but there was a shortage of men. So I started making phone calls to the guys I knew. Nobody took me seriously enough to come. I was frantic. I quickly started making my rounds at the bar. I went from group to group over and over again trying to pay them all equal amounts of attention, buying them drinks, and reassuring them that this wasn't an average night, that it was usually better than this on Wednesdays. I was lying to them, but I wanted them to stay and to come back again in the following weeks.

Even though I was in recovery, and the last place I should have been was in a nightclub, this job was perfect for me. I was constantly consumed with what people thought of me which made me a people pleaser. I didn't drink, and I was still shy and awkward in most social gatherings. However, my constant fear of people having negative views of me kept me busy checking on people, catering to their needs, and making sure they had a good time. My intention was hard to tell by my demeanor. Most people asked why I looked so serious all the time and why I never smiled. I was always on guard, playing the walls of the bars like I played the walls of a prison, watching everything and waiting for something to kick off. It was inherent in my nature, and my ego still had me looking at every other man as if he were a threat, rather than a potential friend. My history with drinking and the way I acted under the influence also had me extremely untrusting of anyone who was intoxicated. I was used to attacking people for no reason when I was drunk, and so I often expected that from others.

When the first night ended, we had enough to pay the DJ and security, and there was only $75 left. Rather than split the money, Mark gave it to me. I tried to argue, after all it was his party and I felt like he should keep it. But he insisted we wouldn't have earned it if not for me. It wasn't the kind of money either of us wanted to be making, but it was a start and a huge improvement from his attempts in previous weeks. Each week the party grew significantly, and soon we were splitting $300 at the end of the night after everyone else was paid.

Throughout these weeks, I still worked at the restaurant, but after work my nights became even more social as I was out promoting the parties. I invested all of my time into the promotions because it was the only way I saw myself getting out of the restaurant business. I hung out at night at bars handing out flyers, or in parking lots of nightclubs to hand them out when the clubs closed, or leave them on cars. Myspace also became a never-ending source of promotion because I could share digital copies of the party flyers and interact with people from all over the city.

A local sports bar and steakhouse in Baltimore County

became a routine hangout for me on Tuesdays and Fridays, and I felt an immediate draw to a beautiful blonde bartender there. She had just the right amount of sassiness and a trace of the streets in her to pique my interest. I began flirting back and forth with her at the steakhouse and talking back and forth over social media until we met in person a few times. I blew off the other women I had been talking to and immediately got comfortable with this new girl, Brielle. She showed an interest in more than just the external me. Most women were attracted to the show I put on and the facades I wore. I still lived at home with my parents, and I still lived week to week waiting tables. However, I had fresh Coogi outfits and sneakers every day of the week. And I adorned myself in gold jewelry and a tough guy attitude like I was the hardest guy in the bar. These things masked my insecurities and attracted women who would have random sex with me, but they would never attract the woman who I would ultimately call my girlfriend.

Brielle, not only fit the mold, but she had herself together a lot more than I did. She had her own apartment, she worked a day job at an insurance company, and she bartended the steakhouse at night. In retrospect, she was out of my league. At the time, even though I had nothing to offer, I had put myself on such a pedestal that I thought any girl was lucky to have me. What really caught my attention was that Brielle noticed other things about me. She noticed my poetry and inquired about it, and she wanted to read more of it. She spoke to me about my potential and how she could see another side of me. Her interest in who I really was changed my habit of completely avoiding relationships at all costs, to cutting off all of my other flings to only be with her.

She had a thing for bad boys though. She had a long

history of dating drug dealers and assorted criminals. My lifestyle had changed, but the persona I hung onto still fit the mold well. I was a steroided-out nightclub promoter who still dressed like a drug dealer. My outer layer was appealing to her, as was my soft, deeper inner layer. We quickly started spending all of our time together, and our mischievous comical natures matched perfectly. We would prank people together, act like goofy kids having fun, and yet she also loved getting dressed up and coming to the nightclub parties with me.

The fifth party I helped promote at the nightclub with Mark fell on Christmas night. I had strong confidence that we would have a great turnout on the night of Christmas because I felt like many people, much like myself, feel kind of empty and lost that night after family leaves and festivities have ended. What better time to go out with friends and show off your new outfits?

I promoted this experimental party fiercely for two weeks leading up to it, and when the time arrived, I was a bundle of excitement and anxiety. I had no idea what to expect. There had been a large party at the same establishment the night before, and the test of my accomplishment was to see if ours could outdo it. It did, but not in a good way.

Like most nightclub parties, we opened the doors around 7 PM, and I stood there frantic as nobody walked through the doors for the first hour. Then people began to trickle in, and by 10 PM we had a line at the door. Mark sat at the table in the lobby with the cash box while Brielle and I stood next to him. I collected money and stamped the backs of people's hands once they paid their cover to Mark. Behind me, a bouncer checked their IDs before letting them into the nightclub. The music thundered throughout the venue, mostly all dance and Hip Hop. Occasionally, I would make my rounds, or cut through to the bathroom, just to gauge our results. The place was packed in no time, and as usual it was wide assortment of people from all over Baltimore and its suburbs. The parties were usually mixed crowds of different colors, nationalities, and walks of life. There were a lot of college kids and preppy kids from the suburbs, as well as older adults, and the usual drug dealers who spent a lot of money in the bar on top shelf liquor. All were welcomed.

As the night grew long, more unfamiliar faces arrived. Brielle pointed to a group of guys I had never seen before and said, "There's going to be trouble in here tonight."

"Pssshhh… I'm not worried about them. They'll be fine," I said, eyeing them up, always keeping my cool image going.

I played the walls of the nightclub the same way I always did. I never smiled, always kept my back to the wall, and watched everything. I was the host and the promoter of the party, and yet people often asked why I never smiled, not even for pictures. I was all business, always serious and always on guard. It was a defense mechanism to protect my own fragility, but was also the response to my own anxiety. At the time I wasn't aware of these things, I just thought I was tough, and that's how tough guys act. The crowd began to look rough. The hip hop, by request, got increasingly more gangster and less dance. I noticed a couple of guys on the dance floor who had taken off their shirts and were now in 'wifebeater' tank tops. I pulled security aside and asked if they were cool with it. The head of security was familiar with them, as was the owner. They sold a lot of cocaine in the area. One of them was awaiting sentencing on drug distribution, and the other had just gotten home from prison.

"They'll be okay", security told me.

Brielle eventually left because she had to work the next morning and reminded me I had my hands full that night. I kissed her goodnight, walked her to her car, and returned to the club. I walked through the club basking in my glory watching the hundreds of people I had managed to bring together having a good time. The bars were lined with young men and women ordering drinks, the dance floor was packed, and I felt accomplished. I walked to the bathroom, and that's when all hell broke loose.

As I came out of the bathroom, Mark came running past me covered in sweat. As he slid across the floor, bottles, glasses, and high heel shoes went soaring through the air in his direction. They crashed and shattered against the walls and floor around him as he ran. He looked scared to death, as the entire club it seemed was charging in his direction looking like they wanted to kill him. He turned and ran and hid in the kitchen, as the bouncers formed a line blocking the hallway that led to the kitchen. I had to scoot past them into the angry crowd of screaming and crying women in order to get back into the club. The music stopped, and the only sound was screaming. One of the guys who was wearing a wifebeater stumbled through the club with blood pouring out of his head like a faucet and gushing down his face. The first thing I could think was, *Damn, Brielle, was right!* I wandered through the club wondering what the hell had just happened to cause such a chaotic scene, meanwhile hoping all of these people didn't associate me with Mark and turn on me.

"He fucking hit me! That little bitch hit me with a bottle!" one of the women screamed through drunken tears.

"I'll kill that motherfucker!" another screamed while taking her heels off to throw at security.

I was mind-blown. Why would Mark hit these girls, and why was he even in a position to do so? The last time I saw him he was at the table counting money. Now the club was in pure disarray. There was blood all over the dancefloor and a trail leading out into the lobby. People were running and screaming in every direction, and the bouncers were dragging people towards the exit who fought back against them.

In the midst of the insanity, my mind went to one thing, and my heart dropped. The cashbox! I knew Mark didn't have it when he ran past me and slid across the floor a few minutes ago. Anyone could have it at this point. I jogged to the lobby, dodging the angry mob, stepping over the blood trail, and keeping my eyes on everyone around me on the way. As I stepped into the lobby where people were emptying out of the club on their own accord, or forcefully by the hands of bouncers, I saw a blood trail leading right out of the front door, tons of flyers scattered everywhere, and there on the floor, randomly sitting out in the wide open—the cashbox. *Somebody had to have looted it and threw it there*, I quickly deduced. I ran over to scoop it up. Sure enough, inside, all of the night's cash was scattered about loosely. Over two thousand dollars, if my math was correct.

I tucked the box under my armpit like a football and walked it to my car and placed it inside. It was the only safe place I could think of. Then I went back in to talk to security and get the scoop. The real chain of events that unfolded while I was in the bathroom was much different than what I was initially presented.

While I was in the bathroom, and only Mark was at the front door, an argument between a boyfriend and girlfriend had broken out in front of the club. The guy punched his girlfriend in her face. Upon seeing this through the club's glass doors, Mark went outside and told the guy to get out of there, that we weren't going to have any beating on women at the party. The guy then punched Mark. Mark's friend, a large black dude named Keyon, saw it and attacked the guy. The guy went to his car and got a crowbar out of the trunk. He danced around the parking lot, waving his crowbar at Mark and Keyon and shouted at them. The guy's brothers were the two guys in wifebeaters, and they came busting out of the doors with a small mob of people. Seeing his posse gave the young guy some extra confidence, and he stepped forward and swung the crowbar at Keyon. Keyon's arms flew up to protect his face, When the crowbar made contact with his forearms, it dropped to the ground and all hell broke loose. Everybody came into a circle, and Mark, the least violent of them all, came up swinging the crowbar and cracked one of the brothers in the forehead, and his head split it open instantly.

Suddenly they all turned their attention towards Mark and charged him, including the girl who had gotten punched in the first place. She screamed that Mark hit her. In turn everybody in the club got fired up, and thus my first Christmas party turned into a bloodbath. It was mayhem. But I wasn't done yet. This was only the beginning.

Recovery had taught me some core principles that had become embedded in my moral fiber. They actually weren't anything new to me. These foundational principles were already at the very core of who I was. I had just cast them aside when I decided at an early age that I didn't like who I was, and I would become something else. But now, through abstinence and doing the things I needed to do in order to successfully live without drugs or alcohol, I was learning how to embrace, albeit very slowly, the person God had intended me to be. For me, this meant there were certain behaviors I could no longer engage in if I wanted to remain sober and well. At the very core of these behaviors was stealing. At a very early age, even before drugs and alcohol, stealing was a way of life for me.

As a young boy, my parents demonstrated that more often than not, 'no' was a more common answer than 'yes' and rightfully so. Most of my friends, however, came from one-parent homes, and I saw how their single mothers overcompensated by giving them everything they wanted and allowing them to do anything they wanted. I learned that if I wanted to compete and fit in, then I had to steal whatever I wanted, and I became very good at it. I became so good in fact, that stealing became second nature to me and almost an addiction in and of itself. I would steal to get what others had, then I would steal to outdo what others had, and then I would steal just to steal. Once I became addicted to drugs, theft became the number one means by which I supported my addiction.

If I were to live a new lifestyle, theft would be the number one thing I would have to cut out of my life after drugs and alcohol had been removed. I imagined God would strike me down if I got clean and continued to live dishonestly. Yet somehow in my warped and egocentric mind, I still managed to justify cheating on previous girlfriends and selling drugs, but I never stole or lied about anything else. Thankfully, once I met Brielle, all those previous behaviors had changed as well.

When I walked back into the kitchen to speak to Mark after the nightclub crowd had been fully dispersed, I did so with the cashbox in hand. I had the fleeting thought of driving away with the two thousand dollars and pretending like it had been stolen. But it was only fleeting. Two thousand dollars was a lot of money to me at the time, but it wasn't worth the sleepless nights and eventual backslide to negative behaviors that would potentially follow.

"It's all there, bro. $2,100," I said proudly, as I handed the box over to an astonished Mark, still wondering in the back of my mind if he'd think I pilfered some.

"I can't do this anymore" he said, exasperated. "Go take care of the DJ and security, and split up the rest."

I did as he said. I felt sorry for him. He wasn't at fault in all of this, but I knew he couldn't come back next week or the week after because retaliation from the crowd was inevitable. Mark dabbled in and knew a lot of people in the streets, but he wasn't built for the street life. He was a businessman and a hustler, always coming up with some kind of borderline illegal scheme to make money, but he certainly wasn't a thug or convict like me or the rest of the people he was up against. I paid off our employees and split the remaining $2,100 between us.

Mark decided to walk away from the entire promotion business and conceded that I was 'better at it anyway'. He told me I could take over the parties from here forward if I wanted to, and that he was out. I held onto the reins for several years after that and did very well. Mark would eventually come work for me many years later at my bail bonds company. The guy whose head had been split with the crowbar ended up doing ten years a few months later for kingpin drug distribution. He is now a good friend of mine and pillar of the treatment community where he has been working for the past several years.

I spent every minute of my downtime with Brielle. We were inseparable, and oddly, my guard wasn't up with her like it had been with women in the past. I carried on promoting parties at the location where the Christmas incident took place and then began approaching other nightclubs around Baltimore County and City. Between my success at undertaking the party promoting endeavor and my flourishing relationship with a woman who was out of my league, my confidence grew. By normal worldly standards I was still a loser with no future, but in my own mind I was becoming somebody. Somebody very important. My life actually started changing for the better.

Self-confidence is one of the most important ingredients for a successful story of sobriety. We often use drugs to run. We run from feelings, from pain, from sadness, and most often, we run from ourselves. The drugs and alcohol are initially used to mask our insecurities, or to make us into a different (and less insecure) person, then the addiction takes hold. Once we get sober and are separated from the drugs and alcohol, we are left with the same version of ourselves we started with. Only now we are even more hopeless and damaged and ultimately even more insecure.

I started to believe in myself. I had people believing in me too, even though it was only as a club promoter or as a boyfriend. It felt good to be recognized and to be able to put my energy into things and accomplish them on my own and be successful. The personal success combined with begin valued for who I really was began to build upon itself, and I grew in confidence instead of ego. Sure, my ego still had a massive stronghold on me, but my new confidence wasn't founded upon lies. Now it was real and based on experience. The more independently successful I became at the tasks I set out to complete, the more tasks I had the confidence to take on. I gained enough self-esteem to approach new club owners, to interact with new people, and most of all, I began to break out of my introverted shell and learn how to socialize with my newfound confidence.

Brielle and I had been dating about three weeks, and my parents had already been putting enormous pressure on me to move out. I was terrified at the thought. I was now 28 years old, still living at my parents' home, and scared to leave. The world still seemed like a place that would swallow me whole and spit me back out like it had done in the past. I didn't make enough money to pay bills regularly. I had a hustle, but not a career. And I knew I couldn't count on that to regularly pay rent and bills. The brand new relationship with Brielle was moving along nicely, but I didn't want to get backed into a corner. And sure, she had her own place, but I didn't want to rely on our relationship for housing and security, especially this early on. I made excuses to my parents. I stalled and floundered to figure out my next move.

Then one morning at 5 AM, I awoke with heart palpitations. My worst fear had been realized. The panic was back. The same terror and depression I had experienced a few years prior was back with a vengeance. Instantly I was wide awake and hyper-aware, laying in my bed while the rest of the world slept. My heart raced, my skin burned, and I tumbled into an abysmal pit of panic and depression. I closed my eyes and prayed for it to disappear. When it didn't, I prayed for death. The panic attack lasted a week and a half, just like the last one. I cried, I froze, I couldn't fight it. My life instantly lost all meaning, and I lost control of my mind and all of my senses. I begged God for mercy from this inexplicable torture inside. I scrambled to figure out what had caused it and continuously came up empty handed. I couldn't talk, I couldn't move, and yet I couldn't sit still. I was frozen in a level of panic and depression that took me straight into the depths of the hell inside of me. Within a few days my mother became visibly frustrated with me. She asked me to help her with a task, and I cried that I couldn't help. A 28-year-old, big, muscular, healthy man, and I couldn't perform the smallest tasks. I was trapped inside a prison of fear and anxiety where every single thought sent shockwaves of panic physically rippling through my body, paralyzing me.

"Just fucking do it!" She snapped at me, which all by itself caused even more excruciating anxiety. I could understand her frustration at not understanding the unexplainable, and yet I was hurt by the callousness and disregard I felt from her in the middle of my trauma. I knew somehow I had to man up or wither away and die, but I would have chosen the latter at that moment ten times out of ten.

On the flip side, Brielle was an angel. I knew at that moment she was in my life for a reason. Just like many years before in my weak state with Maria, I professed my love to Brielle, and I meant it. I called her my guardian angel, and I felt like she was. She was so soft and understanding, and she catered to my weaknesses. She too experienced severe anxiety attacks, but only in the normal sense in which they would come on for twenty minutes and then leave. Even though she had never experienced these two-week-long anxiety attacks, she at least knew what I was feeling, and so I clung to her. I waited all day, suffering in panic at my parents' house, then felt a slight bit of relief when she would arrive after work with her warmth and her smile.

After about two weeks, when the attacks subsided, my parents pressed the need for me to go. They knew I was in good hands. They felt it was time to push me from the nest and see if I flew or fell to the ground, and so they did.

"You've got one week to find somewhere to live. We've given you more than enough time."

"But where do you expect me to go?" I pleaded. "I don't want to move in with Brielle already. It's only been a few weeks, and she doesn't need me mooching off of her."

"Well, you've got to go somewhere, and I suggest you go with her or find somewhere else," was their frank reply.

Upon telling Brielle my dilemma, she invited me to move in with her. "Don't worry, you don't have to pay any bills. Come on, it will be fine!"

Once again, I felt like a complete waste of space and a failure. Brielle had shoebox money left over from a past relationship with a guy who was serving a ten-year sentence in federal prison for drug distribution. She was a professional girl, but he had brought her into his world. After his sentencing he instructed her as to where his money was hidden and to keep most of it. I'm sure he didn't intend on her spending it on me, but she did. During the first few months of our relationship, I was treated like a king. I was never allowed to pay for our dinners or lunches out, and if I tried to pay, I was silenced. I was given gifts and treated way better than I ever deserved. Even though this was something my ego would have had me bragging about in the past, now I just felt shame. I tried to make it up to her by loving her the best I could, both sexually and emotionally. I thought somehow these things would repay her for the sacrifice she made for me.

She didn't smoke, but she let me smoke in her apartment. She worked at an insurance firm during the day and waited tables on the weekend. I sat in her apartment all day playing on Myspace and promoting club parties on social media, and when she returned, it was usually with hot food. I knew deep down inside that I was worthless, so I protected my ego every way I knew how. I did it with fashion, with attention from promoting parties, and with putting my all into my performance in the bedroom. What I didn't realize, like so many times before, was that Brielle saw something in me I didn't see in myself. She saw and was attracted to the superficial layer on the outside of me, but she had been attracted to the deeper me. She had read my poetry and had deep conversations with me and knew there was more than what the surface revealed. However, instead of embracing that, I chose to work on the outer, more shallow part of myself because it was easier.

For a few years, I promoted parties all over Baltimore and its suburbs. I would start a ladies night on a Wednesday at one club, maybe do a thirsty Thursday at another club, and then a Saturday night party at another. I generally had about three parties going each week. The clubs themselves changed quite often because of extraneous circumstances. There was almost a predictable outcome to every party that went like this: the first couple weeks were generally slow, but each week crowds grew as word spread around town. Then the clubs would fill up with young people and tons of attractive young women. There were key people from Baltimore and its suburbs that I looked forward to seeing at the parties. If they came, then I knew the parties would be a success. The problem was that after word of the parties spread out to the college kids, then the young professionals, then it started getting out to the hood, usually around week six. That's when all the drug dealers and gang members of all colors started filtering in. Baltimore County is a mixed bag of white and black low-income neighborhoods, as well as high-income neighborhoods. Thugs come in all colors there, and those were once my people. They were welcomed by the bar owners as well because while some of them were broke, a good bit of them were rolling in money from illegal activities and loved spending it on high dollar drinks at the bar for everyone in their crew.

By the third or fourth month of hosting successful parties, the club owners got tired of mopping blood off the dance floor, or got tired of police getting called and their liquor license being threatened. The fights and stabbings were almost inevitable; the violence came with the territory. Sometimes it was due to the club owner's greed, allowing anyone inside in order to make money, and other times our hands were tied. If you started imposing a serious dress code, you were labeled as a racist establishment and/or alienated a lot of your regulars who weren't trouble makers. It was out of my hands, I was simply there to fill the place up and keep the club patrons happy. I paid the security but they took their orders from the bar owners. That's how I preferred it to be. I was able to justify immoral decisions that way. I promoted to everybody, and when a lot of underage people started showing up, if the owner and security let them in, then that was just more money for me.

At no point did it cross my mind that I was helping to promote the same disease that had destroyed my life. I saw the same people day in and day out, the same people being banned and escorted out by security just like I was many years ago. I watched the same drug dealers who I had become friends with go back and forth to the parking lot with their clientele every night, but I turned a blind eye. They drew money, and so did the alcohol. I was trying to survive, and my ego was in tip-top shape. It was all part of the game. Sometimes a mirror image of the old me would show up to these parties and get drunk and reckless and crack somebody in the head with a bottle or beat someone bloody in the bathroom. Then after we threw them out of the club, I would harm them or encourage somebody else to do it. It never occurred to me that the person I was harming suffered with addiction and insecurity just like the old me did.

My longest running party lasted a few years and took place at the avenue in White Marsh, ten minutes north of Baltimore. This Wednesday ladies night party alone made me around $1,000 a week. When it fell on the night before Thanksgiving, I walked away with $7,000 from just that one night. That was big money to a guy who never made real money legally and who didn't have to work hard for it. It just took a little creativity and a reputation that was quickly spreading. One night, towards the end of the night, a usual troublemaker was being escorted out by security. Brielle was standing out front of the club as he was exiting. He was screaming and cursing and spitting on the windows of the club. I had just finished counting money and was taking the money and cashbox to my car to stash it. As I exited the club, I heard Brielle talking kindly to him, "Why don't you just calm down and go home for the night?"

Then I heard his response, "Why don't you just suck my dick?" he snarled.

I froze up, "Hey! What did you just say, pussy?" I barked, and he turned eyes glaring and took one step forward. I crammed the cashbox into his forehead. Then, instantly dropping the empty cashbox, I stepped back and squared up. "Come on pussy! Come on pussy!" I repeated. As I did, blood erupted from his forehead. The next response wasn't what I had expected.

This tattooed, tough-guy meth-head, who had been in numerous fights in my clubs broke down and screamed out, "Security!!!!" And he kept screaming it.

There were mall police across the street from the club, and he was running towards them. I scooped up the cashbox and told Brielle I'd see her at home. I ran through the club, through the kitchen, and out the backdoor, hopped in my car and took off. I was sure I was going back to jail.

The guy, like so many others in the area, didn't know my real name. He only knew me as Danny Diamond. So when he went to the police station to file a report, they told him that no such person existed and that he'd need my real name in order to do so. He contacted the club and spoke to the owner, and they pretended not to know my name. For almost a week, he frequented the avenue in White Marsh looking for me so he could call the police and asking around about my real name. I thought I was safe, but weeks later he found out, and I received a notice to appear in court on assault charges.

Brielle and I had moved into a rental townhouse on the water. Of course with my tarnished credit and my criminal history, I couldn't go on the rental agreement. I had to stay there covertly. Luckily one of the women who worked at the rental office had a son in a similar situation as me, so we made it our little secret. While Brielle worked all day, I fished out back. When she came home I was usually on the couch playing video games or on the pier nearby fishing. I had picked up a lot of weight since being off of steroids and not working out. All the bulk I had gained in my chest and shoulders was now hanging out in my midsection. At the time I didn't realize how out of shape I had actually gotten. I spent a lot of time on social media promoting parties and messaging back and forth with people. The goal was to get attractive women into the parties and the rest would fall into place. This began leading to a lot of tension between me and Brielle. She began reading my messages on Facebook and my emails, hovering over me at the door to the nightclubs, and scowling at every pretty girl who talked to me or gave me a welcome hug.

While we had our completely separate lives, we still had our common interests and our shared sense of humor. So even as her friends and coworkers told her how I was a loser and she could do better, she was still drawn to me and attached to me. Our sex life began to fade out, and a certain level of animosity existed between us just below the surface. She read some flirtatious messages between me and other women, women who were no doubt interested in sleeping with me, and I was always one to be overtly friendly for the sake of my business. This added to the underlying turmoil. We held on though, trying to make things work, but we were both growing increasingly unhappy with one another. I had nowhere to go if I left, and I think she felt equally trapped and had pity on me because of this.

Months went by and the court case finally came for the assault charge. I doubted the kid who was pressing charges would even show up. He was a criminal and a wanna-be tough guy himself. I couldn't imagine he would be standing in a courtroom, muscles bulging, covered in tats, and telling a judge he was assaulting people at a party and had gotten thrown out, and then I hit him with a cashbox. I figured his pride wouldn't bring him into a courtroom, but sure enough when I arrived he was already there. Something was different though... he was skinnier, and I could tell immediately by his eyes that he was high on heroin. Now it all made sense. He wanted money. I had an attorney who regularly sponsored my parties come and represent me for free.

I pulled my attorney aside and said, "I can't believe he's here, not only that, but he's visibly doped up." I pointed him out to my attorney. "Listen, try this," I said, looking around the courtroom. "See if you can pull him aside and offer him two hundred bucks to drop this ridiculous case." It was a sting to my pride to give him anything and fall prey to his game, but I couldn't afford more charges or to potentially go back to jail after all this time.

My lawyer spoke to the state's attorney, then walked out of the courtroom with the victim. When they came back in, my lawyer nodded at me and walked back over to the state's attorney and spoke into her ear. When I saw her nod, I breathed a sigh of relief. He returned to me, looking serious and stern despite the fact I knew it was resolved.

"Do you have it on you?" he asked.

"Of course, I do," I replied, already reaching into my pocket. I counted out two hundred dollars and handed it to him. He walked back out of the courtroom with the victim, then waived me out after the kid left. I felt sorry for the guy in spite of everything. I had just given him money to go get high, but I was in survival mode. I had to protect myself first, I thought. I left the courthouse that day feeling victorious and yet dirty at the same time. At no point in my life had I ever walked into a courtroom with a dime to my name, let alone enough to pay off the accuser. It was a good day for me, yet I didn't feel right about it. I shouldn't be in these situations anymore to begin with. I still had some growing up to do.

During my exploits promoting clubs, I had reached out to a lot of businesses in the area, most of which were owned by ex-drug dealers and street dudes who had gone legit. They ranged from auto-detailers, to rim shops, to bail bondsmen. I had gone to the same guy who owned a bail bonds company to promote every single party. Whether it was a bikini contest or regular weekly party, I knew I could count on them for two hundred to several hundred dollars in sponsorship money. This bought them access to come hand out merchandise and advertise at the event. I also became friends with an older black dude named Billy Greene who had been promoting parties for quite a long time in the same areas and to the same general crowd that I was. We clicked immediately, and rather than compete, we ended up teaming up on a lot of projects together. He also ran a nightclub security crew and had his own DJs, which was beneficial. Most of all, I really enjoyed our weekly lunches together when we would discuss the politics of the local scene, gossip, and discuss further life ambitions.

Because of my paranoia, I kept Billy at arm's length. The industry was cutthroat like any other business, and even though we teamed up often, we also had our own separate parties. We dipped into the same pools of DJs, sponsors, and clientele. I had to stand my ground often, and we would occasionally have a small falling out over things. He knew I wouldn't back down, and he repeatedly told me and others how he respected my grind and knew I would be successful. I was too proud to admit it at the time, but he was something like a mentor to me, one I wouldn't let get close enough to fully trust. After all, it was Billy, who after repeatedly telling me how good I would be at bail bonds, ultimately pushed me in that direction. He encouraged me to go talk to Sammy about getting into the bail bonds business, and that's what I did.

Sammy had a highly successful bail bonds company in

Baltimore, among other businesses in the past, but had to sell it before he did ten years with the feds for kingpin distribution. After he came home from his sentence, he opened up another bail bonds business in Baltimore County, and it became highly successful. His marketing and promotion was top notch, and he spent hundreds of thousands of dollars on it every year. He saw me hustling on a much smaller scale to promote the clubs over the years, and he agreed I had big potential in the bail bonds industry. He decided to show me how to start my own bail bonds business. I would be writing my bails through his insurance policy, and he would be getting a small cut, of course.

I already had a plan. He had Baltimore County and the city pretty much covered, however I had grown up a little north in Harford County, and I felt like I knew enough people there to get a solid foothold in the game. Like most ideas that come to me, when I become passionate about it, my creative juices flowed in overdrive. I immediately had a vision of where I wanted my office to be, what my company name was going to be, and what colors and logo I was wanted to use. Freedom Fighters Bail Bonds was born almost overnight. The skeleton key in my logo was the key to freedom, not only for those who were incarcerated, but also for me: to be free of my past, free of this lifestyle of club promoting, and to be free to earn some real legitimacy in the world.

LEVEL SIX

This might not be an easy time
There's rivers to cross and hills to climb
Some days we might fall apart
And some nights might feel cold and dark
When nobody wins afraid of losing
And the hard roads are the ones worth choosing
Some day we'll look back and smile
And know it was worth every mile

—Chris Stapleton

HINDSIGHT IS 20/20, and I could list a hundred more cliches to describe the course of my life. Every single event that seemed to make absolutely no sense at the time has led me to exactly where I'm supposed to be. My stumbling blocks were actually stepping stones. My struggles were opportunities for growth. My mistakes were lessons learned. My external triumphs weren't really successes at all, but rather actual victories happening in my soul and spirit that I was unaware of at the time. I was still being forged by fire.

Every relationship, every friendship, every hustle I stepped into, every bit of trouble I found—they were all a piece of the path I was meant to be on. God could get through to a hard head like mine slowly and gradually. Brielle was a huge boost at a time in my life when I was lost and stuck. I will never forget her for that, but there eventually came a time when I like to think that she outgrew me, but in actuality we outgrew each other. I could have never managed the next stage of my life and a relationship at the same time, and she was moving quickly in another direction. She was a blessing to me, and will always be an angel in my life. I hope I also played a role in showing her what she really wanted and didn't want from a relationship. Inadvertently, we were both were teachers.

I took the few thousand dollars I had and found the exact location I wanted for my bail bonds office in downtown Bel Air, Maryland. Bel Air is a small suburb about 20 miles north of Baltimore. My first choice for my new office was right on the main corner of town directly next to the Circuit Courthouse. When I envisioned myself opening a bail bonds office, I had a clear picture of what I wanted in my mind, and then I went out and found it. There were very few times in my life in which I had clear visions of what I wanted, but when I was 100% sure, I found that they always came just like I envisioned. Never immediately, but in due time.

In this case I took an underground office beneath the office I actually wanted. The underground office was extremely cheap, dark and damp, and afforded me almost no visibility from the street. However, it was what I could afford at the time, and close enough to where I wanted to be. Within my first year, the tenant above me moved out, and I moved up to the large street level corner office with huge glass windows and tons of visibility. I was right where I had imagined I would be.

The office was a thirty-minute drive from where Brielle and I lived, and within weeks of opening, the engine in my car went out. After work one day, Brielle was happy to go car shopping with me. I couldn't afford any of the big trucks or cars that all the other bail bondsmen drove like big pickups, Hummers, and Escalades, although it was my vision to get a white one and wrap it in red, white, and blue with the logo and phone number all over it. Instead, I tried to buy what I could afford, a tiny black Nissan Sentra. Financing immediately put a stop to the purchase. I had very little money to put down, terrible credit, and no proof of income. I don't know where

I ever got the idea that I could purchase a car. I was stuck. I walked out of the finance office with my head down.

"What's wrong?" Brielle asked.

"They're not going to let me buy the car unless I have a co-signer. I don't know what the fuck I'm gonna do," I said, exhausted.

"Well, what do you want to do?" she asked, not taking the bait.

"I don't know, I can try my parents, but I seriously doubt they will. I just got the bail bonds business opened, and this happens. Figures, it's the story of my life!" I sighed.

"Fine!! God damnit!" She snapped and stormed into the finance office.

We had been at odds a lot lately, but I had rarely ever seen her this mad at me. She was shaking as she spoke to the finance manager and handed over her driver's license.

I followed after her. "You don't have to do this. I'll try to get my father to, I'm not forcing you…" I felt horrible, but stunned. Things had definitely changed. This wasn't the same girl who would do absolutely anything for me in the beginning.

She had tears streaming down her face as she signed the paperwork. "I'll do this, but I swear to fucking God, Danny, if you don't pay this, I'm done! I'm done!"

I knew she had been through this before. I knew what had been done to her, and I didn't want to be another burden on her life. She had been through a relationship previously where she signed for a guy's car and motorcycle, and not only did he never make payments and ruin her credit, but she caught him sleeping in their bed with numerous women. *I'm not him*, I thought to myself, *I would never do that to her*. But, honestly, I didn't know what tomorrow brought. How did I know whether the bail bonds business would succeed or fail? It hadn't even started yet. What if the weekly parties completely stopped? They were already dying out. Again, like so many times before, I was in survival mode. I was completely dependent on another person in order to survive and stay afloat, and I hated it. I hated being a burden on anyone, especially the woman I loved, but I needed it. I had a clear vision of my future and success, and I couldn't let something like this stop me so early in the game. *I'll prove to everyone what I can accomplish*, I reasoned.

It wasn't an H2 Hummer, but I was proud of it. I immediately took that little car to the graphics shop and got it wrapped in big red, white, and blue stickers representing the bail bonds company logo and phone numbers. I parked it right on Main St in Bel Air out front of my office to make up for the lack of storefront I had. And I sat. I sat in that office all day, most days scouring the internet for free ways to advertise and get publicity. I looked for open cases and cross referenced, trying to locate the families of people in need of bails. For days, then weeks, I sat there trying to figure out how to make my phone ring. Once it finally did, it never stopped.

I'll never forget my first bail. I sat in the courtroom for bail review taking notes. When they read off the inmates addresses, I jotted it down. Then I went back to my office and started cross referencing addresses to try to get telephone numbers. This was in 2010, when few landlines were still in existence, and cell phone numbers weren't listed. However, one day I called and connected with a man whose son was incarcerated on a $20,000 bail. I finally got a live person on the phone, but I was nervous. I didn't want to mess up my chance. I started explaining who I was and the reason for my call, and the response wasn't quite what I expected.

"Oh great! I was about to start looking for a bail bondsman," was the older gentleman's response. I explained the process and gave him the address to my office. Waiting on the edge of my seat to see if he would show up before getting redirected somewhere else in the process, I finally saw his legs coming down the stairs to my office. I drew up the paperwork with him, collected the money, and posted the bail. That was the smoothest $1,600 dollars I had ever made. I started doing the math in my head to see how much I could make if I did just one of those a day. His was my first bail in three months, but at least it paid two months of rent in my tiny little underground office.

Not every bail was going to be as smooth as the first one. In Maryland the law is that you collect 10% on any bail you write. A bail is insurance that an inmate shows up for court. When a person is arrested for a crime and is facing time in jail, then there is no real assurance they will show up for their court date. Since there is no penalty for not showing up to court, and since technically you are innocent until proven guilty, there is no justifiable way to hold people in jail who are awaiting court unless they've proven to be an extreme flight risk or danger to the community. The amount of bail assigned to a person is also weighed upon those two factors: risk of flight and potential danger to themselves or others. For example, a person charged with their first or second DWI will most likely be released, but a third or fourth (or more) offense will probably land them a bail, in higher increments depending upon the number of times they offended.

Our insurance company put the money up to cover the full bail amount. We just did the marketing, promoting, record keeping, and paperwork, as well as posting the actual bails.

We were the middleman between the inmate and their loved ones and the insurer. Sammy had a contract with an insurer. As such, he was liable for catching anyone who skipped bail. On any bail that I wrote, I owed Sammy a percentage off the top, and he then owed a percentage of that to the insurance company. The arrangement was perfect for me because I didn't have to bounty hunt or hire bounty hunters. Sammy had a vast network of bail bondsmen all over the state working under him with the same agreement as me. This allowed me to focus on making new money and not spend time chasing lost money. He had full time bounty hunters for that. He gave me an opportunity I may have never had, and I wanted to show my appreciation. I wanted to make him grateful that he put his trust in me. I wanted to make myself a lot of money, but I also wanted to make him a lot as well.

There was a catch though. His ultimate marketing strategy to take over bail in the state was to start financing bails. The Maryland Insurance Agency, our regulatory overseer, required us to attempt to collect 10% on all bails. But there was no law saying that the 10% couldn't be financed. Sammy started advertising 1% down on all bails, and it completely changed the game. Before long, every other bail bondsman was forced to adapt and start doing the same, or face going out of business. Further, the judges and court commissioners who regularly set bails began to see that people were now getting out of jail on 1% down, so they began setting higher bails. Now, instead of setting a $10,000 bail on an assault charge and knowing the person needed $1,000 to be released, they were intentionally setting $100,000 bails knowing that the person still needed the same $1,000 to be released. The problem was that on the $100,000 bail, the accused and the person who signed for them still owed another $9,000 according to law (rather than $900 on a $1,000 bail). It wasn't long before half the city was in debt to one or more bail bondsman. It wasn't uncommon to look up a person's record in the civil database and see they had judgements from several bail bondsmen. I'm not just talking about criminals either. I'm talking about working class mothers and wives, who repeatedly signed for their inmates and never paid the bails.

That was the other problem. Very rarely did anyone in the industry actually pay the money they owed. I'd estimate maybe 1 in 5 actually paid off the bail. That made it hard for us little guys because we were taking 1% down, but owed Sammy 2% off the top. So, if I was doing a $100,000 bail for 1% down, then I was starting out $1,000 in the red, knowing there was only a 20% chance that people would actually pay. When they didn't pay, their files were sent to lawyers for collections who were rarely ever able to collect. The reason for this was the lack of stability in the community that we dealt with. We tried to get reliable cosigners, but reliable people generally weren't interested in cosigning for a bail. They'd usually try to pawn that responsibility off on a family member with nothing to lose. If we waited or asked for too many requirements from the signer in regards to the bail, they would just go to one of our competitors. It was a rat race and an absolute feeding frenzy. On top of that, as commissioners and judges began handing out higher bails and other people saw the bail bondsmen out marketing heavily, then more people wanted to get into the industry. Soon there were hundreds of small bail bonds companies throughout the city and its suburbs competing fiercely for bails, which ultimately meant lower down payments and worse quality cosigners.

To make matters worse, a lot of these smaller bail bondsmen didn't have money in the bank to take the initial loss when financing a bail, so instead of offering a low down payment, they broke the law and offered a low flat fee. Maryland state law was that we had to charge 10% on a bail, whether we took a low down payment or got it all up front. Now there were hundreds of bail bondsmen out there, many of whom were unlicensed, operating strictly off of their cellphones, and had no offices or other operational costs, so they were undercutting everyone. This happened because another notorious Baltimore drug dealer was doing exactly what Sammy was doing, but doing it completely unethically and allowing anyone to write bails under him. At one time there was a 'bail bondsman' on almost every block in Baltimore. They were charging a flat fee as low as 2.5% on bails. And if they made $50 to $100 profit a day, they were happy because they had no bills associated with a business to pay. It was an all-out feeding frenzy, but it was a numbers game. The more bails you wrote, the more you controlled the market, and the more your company's name became a household name in the community.

I can't imagine what went through my parents' heads when I told them that I was opening a bail bonds company or how seriously they took it at first, but they showed their full support. Maybe they saw the belief I had in my dream and the passion I had to succeed. Maybe they could feel it. Anything was probably better in their eyes than club promoting or even waiting tables for the rest of my life. This was nothing that I ever in a million years dreamed I'd be doing. I never expected to live past 21, then 25, let alone 30. I'd been in and out of jails and prisons 29 separate times. This was definitely something I never expected. But it was a wave. It was a wave that seemed to come out of nowhere, and I knew it was my chance. It was my *kairos. Kairos* is a word I embraced throughout my life and used many times. It is a Greek word for time. However, there are two Greek words for time, one is *chronos* and the other is *kairos. Chronos* is the chronological concept of time as we think of it, and the normal meaning of time. *Kairos* is the exact moment in time when things happen, an exact moment that can determine everything that follows. It is crucial. It was my one opportunity to either catch the wave or be swept in by it.

So I dove into the bail bonds industry. At one point it basically became my religion. I went to sleep with my phone in my hand and woke up the same way. Nights on the couch watching movies with Brielle became a nightmare for her because I spent the entire night on the phone talking bails and often had to rush out at any given moment to do paperwork. The same went for our dinner dates; it was as if this woman across the table from me didn't even exist. My livelihood, my whole world, was attached to that cellphone. I could see nothing except becoming a success for once in my life, and nothing else mattered. My relationship was already on the rocks, but now it suffered horribly. There was no sex, no romance, and hardly any interaction, just a strong underlying current of animosity. To her, I was an ungrateful waste of space in her life who no longer showed her attention or appreciation. I tried, but the business wouldn't let me. I was consumed with the idea of finally being successful, finally standing on my own two feet and not relying on her or anyone else to pay the bills or support me in any way. The business was my entire life, and my future was at stake.

I was still hanging onto the parties. They still fueled my ego and provided me with guaranteed weekly cash, and now

I could even use them to promote my bail bonds company instead of someone else's. They weren't my primary focus anymore, but I still put effort into them because they would help establish my bail bonds company and fuel the costs for further marketing.

Brandon Novak from the TV show *Jackass* was a regular at one of my weekly parties. He would sit at the bar by himself and drink red wine all night. I approached him about being the guest of honor at a Cinco De Mayo party I wanted to host at a new bar I hadn't promoted before. He agreed, and we decided to have him pull one of his ridiculous stunts at the event to help draw hype. His idea of a stunt was to come zip lining naked into the bar, but the owner wasn't having it. His second idea was to do a raffle and the winner would get to tattoo him right there at the party that night.

"What do you want to have them tattoo on you?" I asked.

"I don't know, I'll think of something," he said.

I couldn't believe this guy was going to let some random stranger mark up his body with something that would be there for the rest of his life. The guy who won the raffle that night ended up tattooing "Cinco De Faggo" on Brandon's arm in what looked like childish scribble. I was appalled.

That night, Brielle and I stood at the front door collecting money and watched the place fill up. It was a rough crowd, and I expected a lot of drama before the end of the night. At one point, Brielle and I were standing in a crowd on the sidewalk out front of the bar when we heard a loud commotion. Three girls were being thrown out of the club and were trying to fight with the bouncers to get back in. They had apparently smashed a bottle over another girl's head in the ladies room and were jumping her before security was able to snatch them up and get them out. Brielle was rolling her eyes and talking about how trashy they were when one of them stumbled into her. She spun around, and thinking they were coming for her, Brielle punched the girl in her face. Suddenly all three of them were on her, attacking her. Females or not, I couldn't watch them all pile onto my girlfriend. I wasn't about to stand helplessly watching Brielle get pulverized. I punched one in the back of her head and sent her reeling, then grabbed another and threw her into a bush out front of the club. I was ready to fight these women like men. I felt like it was my duty to protect Brielle. As I squared off with them, they began to back off.

Brielle was pissed off. I knew this would be a long night, and an added strain on our relationship. She didn't belong in these kinds of parties; she only came because of me. The fact of the matter was that I didn't belong in these kinds of parties anymore either. I didn't drink, I didn't use drugs, and I certainly didn't sell drugs anymore. I had no business being in these places, let alone promoting them. I promised myself and Brielle that once the bail bonds was making steady revenue, then the parties would be done.

It wasn't easy to let go, though. I was addicted to the attention, the hustle, and the rush of creating something out of nothing and watching it grow. The next night I had another party across town, and Brielle made it clear that she wasn't coming and probably wouldn't be coming to anymore after that. I stood at the door alone for once. I felt a small amount of freedom, but also a sense of sadness because I knew things were spiraling to an end. I stamped hands, collected money, and watched as the bar overflowed with people dancing and having a good time, but I felt empty inside.

At one point a group of guys were thrown out for starting

fights, so security and I stood out front exchanging words, ready to fight with them. One of them threatened to come back and shoot all of us. I had grown used to these threats; they were almost expected. Later in the night, a girl came walking in and her jaw dropped when she saw me. It was one of the girls from the night prior, specifically the one I had punched in the back of the head.

"Danny, look I'm—"

I cut her off, motioning to security. "She can't come in," I snapped.

"What's wrong?" they asked, so I explained the events of the night before.

She pleaded, "Danny, it wasn't me. It was the other girls who did all that shit. They're not with me tonight. I'll be fine, I promise."

I just stood there.

"Look, you put a fucking knot in the back of my head. Feel it," she turned around and lifted up her hair to show me the bump. "I'm not mad," she continued, "I know I was wrong. I'm not pressing charges or anything. Just let me in."

I started to feel bad. "Okay, come on, but I swear to God, don't pull any bullshit. And those other girls better not show up here."

The rest of the night went well. I drove home and went into the house quietly. Brielle had to get up early for work, and it often took me awhile to wind down from the adrenaline of the party, and so as not to wake her I would sleep on the couch downstairs. It had become customary. We were rarely sleeping in the same bed anymore.

Just as I started drifting off, her voice startled me, "How was it at the club? Any problems?"

"Nope, it was smooth. But you'll never guess who showed up tonight?"

"Who?" she asked incredulously.

"One of the girls from last night. Can you believe the nerve?" I started, as she cut me off.

"And you let her in didn't you?" she said sharply.

"Yeah, because—"

"You motherfucker!" She shrieked and spit in my face as I lay there talking to her half asleep.

I jumped up off the couch in an instant rage. I wanted to hit her, but I stopped myself. "I'm done. I'm fucking done," I said, laying back down on the couch. "Tomorrow I'm gone."

It took me a little over a week to establish a plan and a new place to live, and so I stayed there in the interim. She left the ball in my court, and I suspect she didn't think I was really leaving. Part of me wasn't sure whether I should. The idea of being able to focus on my future success with zero need to focus on her or anything else is what gave me the extra push to leave there and never look back. My heart was broken and would stay broken for some time, but I knew how to heal it. I'd heal it the same way I always did, by feeding my ego.

I found out very quickly how nearly impossible it was to obtain an apartment with any kind of criminal record. I now owned and operated a bail bonds company, but could not rent an apartment. I didn't have time to shop around for private house rentals either because I had to be out of the house with Brielle within a week. I went directly to an apartment complex just outside of Bel Air and just two miles from my office. The community was built when I was a kid, and we all hung out there as teenagers. It was a higher-end place at the time with a community center and a pool. If I was going to be single, I thought I'd better make my nest somewhere nice. One of the front office people was a friend of mine from my days in the streets. When I walked in and saw him, I was relieved. I thought for sure he could pull some strings for me, but he couldn't. I had to ask my father to put the apartment in his name and pretend like it was his. They couldn't know I lived there. Well, no one but my friend, that is.

I moved my things out of Brielle's, which was absolutely nothing except my clothes and hygiene products. I slept on the floor of the empty apartment for a couple of nights, then on an air mattress for a couple of weeks. The bails were flowing though, and I was running all day, making money hand over fist. Not only was my heart in it, but my soul as well. I hustled all day from sun up to sun down, like my life depended on it.

Bail became very similar to selling drugs. I was dealing with the same exact clientele, going to the same exact neighborhoods, and working out of my car all day long. In order to stay competitive in that cutthroat industry, you had to be willing to do whatever it took to win the bail, which meant not only cutting your cost, but going to people to have them sign and pay rather than waiting for them to come to you. If I waited for them to come to my office, they would likely get called by five other bail bondsmen and be intercepted on the way. So I got up early to head to the city, and usually went back and forth between Baltimore City and various counties making house calls all day long.

The irony was that I was going back to the very same neighborhoods and blocks I used to depend on for my heroin habit, only now I was providing a service to them instead of vice versa. All of that money I gave to drug dealers during the first half of my life was finally coming back to me. I was also walking in and out of the same jails I had been incarcerated in time and time again, only now I was getting people out. The whole routine seemed like a dream. I was on top of my small little world. I lost sight of my recovery, but also my depression and anxiety. My new career received my entire focus, and the more money I made, the more I honed in on the cycle. Drug use, addiction, and my past life wasn't even a viable threat in my mind. I was riding a cloud of success and self-esteem. I felt there was nothing that could pull me down.

The party promotion fell almost completely to the wayside. I only had one weekly party left at a place called Catches on Route 40 in Baltimore County. Every Wednesday night I filled that place with people dancing to Hip Hop, playing beer pong, and of course, selling drugs. The owner would hang out upstairs in his private suite with a couple girls and a couple drug dealers and blow cocaine all night. Since this was his only successful weeknight and opportunity to make money off the bar through the week, he didn't care who security let in. As usual, I stood at the front door minding my own business collecting money and usually ducked out before 1 AM to avoid any craziness.

The last night I was there, we didn't even make it to midnight before a huge brawl started in the front parking lot. It looked like the entire club was out front fighting. The fight had started between a bunch of Edgewood blood members and another group of inner-city guys, and somehow everyone chose a side. When I walked out to see the insanity, it looked like a war zone. People were picking up boulders from a rock garden out front that probably weighed 15-20 pounds each and throwing them at each other's heads. I winced, knowing one of those could kill someone. I came down the steps yelling, "Whoa, whoa, whoa!" to get attention so I could try to calm things down. Just as I did, a bunch of squad cars came squealing into the parking lot with red and blue lights flashing. I started walking backwards up the same steps I had just run down. I watched as boulders bounced off of the hoods of police cars. Some people ran, some people ignored the police, and some antagonized them. I hid inside and waited it out. As the parking lot thinned out and the police wrapped up their arrests, I walked to my car and made my way home. *That will probably be my last night at that location,* I thought to myself.

Two days later people began sending me pictures of an article from the local Baltimore newspaper about me. Not only did it say that I was 'gang affiliated' but that I hosted 'gang parties.' It was clearly over-exaggerated media hype, but there was nothing I could do about it. It wasn't as if I was operating a legitimate tax paying business. Maybe if I wasn't consumed with bail bonds, I would have tried to pursue new venues, but it wasn't worth it anymore. I had a new focus.

The nail in the coffin was when I took one more shot at promoting at an arcade in Harford County, of all places, for my birthday. It was a costume party, and a couple hundred people showed up, and none of them were troublemakers. However, a competitor bar called the liquor board claiming that I was having another 'gang party.' The party was clean and above board, but the liquor board showed up and walked through the dance floor harassing and interviewing people. The next day there was a write up in the local newspaper about my party and how the liquor board observed gang activity. The closest thing to gang activity were a couple people dressed up as ninjas for Halloween. Meanwhile the nightclub that called the liquor board on me had several stabbings that same night. Such is the irony of life.

I was making more money than I ever had at bail bonds. I hired an older lady to do my collections because I had created a lot of revolving debt from writing low money down bails. The common theme went like this: People could literally be standing in front of me with thousands in cash, and I could offer them two options. I would say something like, "You have two options. Give me $600 down now, and owe me nothing. Or give me $300 down now, but you're signing to agree to pay me $2,500." They would choose the payment plan every time, even if they had the money. I joked that I could say, "Give me $200 and owe me nothing more. Or give me $100, and owe me $10,000." And they would choose the $100 every single time. This is because most of them had no intention of paying. Even those with great jobs. I was shocked at how many nurses, business owners, correctional officers, paralegals, etc. would sign and never make a single payment. The problem, of course, was that if I didn't finance the bail, they would just go to the next person who did, and I would lose my branding and reputation.

In 2010-2013 when the bail bonds business was at its height, it was a mostly cash business. On any given day I was walking through the projects of Baltimore with several thousand dollars cash in my pocket. I remember specifically walking to the top floor of a building in Latrobe projects with both pockets bulging with cash. I was picking up $2,000 and already had $10,000 on me. People got killed over $20 around there regularly. And so it went, day in and day out. I felt almost invincible. I convinced myself that when people saw me pull up in my bail bonds car, they knew I was doing a service for the community, but they also probably assumed I was carrying a concealed gun. My criminal record would never allow it, but they didn't know that. I also had a decade of experience on the city streets that made me adept in my surroundings and the actions of the people within them. I exhibited no fear, which was the main thing that saved me.

Many times, I walked into house calls where dope was being cut up in the next room. One time, I walked into a project building in the county and sat at a kitchen table that had a massive pile of raw heroin at the other end. It disgusted me. The only thing that heroin could do was destroy the dream I was chasing. People had no fear of the bail bondsman, and it shocked me. Guns and drugs were everywhere on quite a few of the house calls I would make, and sometimes, I would even say something like, "Man, y'all better be careful. How do you automatically assume I'm cool? I mean, I'd never say nothing, but damn you don't know who you're potentially dealing with."

They'd just snicker, or say something like, "Oh, you the bail bondsman. We know you cool."

At that point in my life, I can honestly say there was zero temptation to go back into my previous lifestyle. There was not one minuscule thing I found appealing about doing heroin again.

Brielle and I had one last tie together I had forgotten about: the car. I was paying the monthly bill, but I hadn't stopped to think that it was still a stressor in her life. She was doubtful about my potential success in the bail industry when I first undertook it, and she had no idea how well I was actually doing. So when she called to ask when I was going to take the car out of her name and put it in somebody else's, I replied, "How about I just pay the whole $17,000 off?"

She sounded completely doubtful. "Yeah, okay Dan. Just do something. I don't want it in my fucking name anymore."

I paid it off the next day, and I was beaming when I called to tell her. I had never been able to do anything like that in my life, nor did I ever think I'd be able to. Next I went to furniture stores. I walked into the furniture store nearby by my apartment complex with $10,000, and tried to buy an $1,800 sofa. They asked if I wanted to finance it, so I said "sure." However, when I got to the counter, they denied me financing because of my credit. I just wanted to build credit, so I asked if I could put half down and finance the rest, and they still said "no."

At this point I was annoyed and cocky. So, I pulled the huge wad of money out of my pocket and said, "I have $10,000 in my pocket and plenty more in the bank, and I can't finance $900 to help build my credit?"

The young girl looked helpless and confused. "I know, it's not your fault."

I lowered my voice, "It's just frustrating, you know?"

I paid cash for the sofa, a few other items, and the extra fee for delivery and assembly. My little 3rd floor apartment was now fully furnished, and I had money in the bank. It was time, I figured, that I start dating again.

For about a year I ran myself ragged. I would wake up at 6am with the phone ringing and run all day. I'd get home at midnight and fall asleep face first in bed with my clothes still on. I awoke throughout the night to answer the phone, and then I was back at it again. Sometimes I went days without showering. I didn't care because I was addicted to the money. It was ten times better than anything else I had ever been addicted to. I bought all brand name designer shoes, belts, and clothing, and I'd show them off on social media, but rarely ever wore them. My daily travels consisted of comfortable sweat clothes to wear in and out of rowhomes in the hood. I traded in the Nissan Sentra and bought a bright blue Cadillac Escalade with huge 38-inch chrome rims. I couldn't bring myself to put bail bonds stickers all over it, even though that had been my initial dream. It was embarrassing for me and my date when I would pick up a woman for the first time and my car looked like a bail bonds billboard. I had dated an older, beautiful Black woman for a while, and one of the reasons we stopped talking is that she couldn't bring herself to be seen in my Nissan Sentra covered in bail bonds advertisements.

My social life consisted of me sitting and eating dinner at the bar of whatever high-end restaurants were nearby at night when I got hungry. I did this in hopes that magically I would meet a beautiful woman. Often I sat at the bar eating dinner, ordering water, juggling phone calls, and trying to make eye contact with the pretty women there. They would have to come to me though; I was still too shy to approach any of them. My ego wouldn't allow me to set myself up for a possible rejection. Besides, I would justify, they were drinking and I was sober. I would make sure I checked in on social media at the nice restaurants where I dined so people would know I had money and good taste. I believed it made me appear mysterious and sophisticated. I was still an insecure young boy trapped in a growing body who had no idea what my real purpose was. I had found a new addiction. Money afforded me the capability to protect myself with financial security and superiority.

I rarely ever spoke about my addiction or my past. I would

mention it upon first meeting a woman in order to protect myself in case they heard things about me, but it never scared them away. The only place I successfully met women was online. We would meet up for a few dates, sleep together a few times, then I would lose interest and we would grow apart. There were never hard feelings. It was usually agreed upon that one or both of us were just too busy for a relationship. The truth was that at my age, almost every woman I dated already had children from another man, and I was far from ready to assume that responsibility.

Then in early 2011, I thought I had everything going for me in life. I had achieved every single goal that I never dreamed I could. I was independent, had nice things, my own place, almost $100,000 in the bank, a luxury car, and hadn't touched drugs in 8 years or alcohol in nearly 13. The only thing missing was a good woman.

There honestly wasn't room for a woman in my life at that time. I couldn't see that though, so like every good addict and egomaniac, I became obsessed with what I couldn't seem to acquire. I had been dating many different women, but never really got serious with one. My dates usually remarked about how shy and quiet I was. I just couldn't seem to break out of my shell. Meanwhile, they all had the social lubricant of alcohol to loosen them up. While I sat at the table sipping my water, they almost inevitably had their wine.

I convinced myself that I could drink again. I had obviously reached the pinnacle of success. *I am a new man*, I rationalized. So one night on a date at a local restaurant, I ordered a glass of red wine. My date knew my history but didn't try to stop me. In fact, she encouraged it, like most of them did because they didn't understand alcoholism or addiction. The craziest thing happened though. I drank that glass of wine and felt amazing. My body warmed up, I smiled more, and I floated through our conversation. I rode home that night with an underlying current of anxiety and confusion, but an overwhelming feeling of triumph. *I am cured.* For the first time in my life I had one drink, acted like an adult, drove myself home at an early hour and went to sleep before midnight. *Holy shit. Hallelujah! I am cured!*

LEVEL SEVEN

And everything I can't remember
As fucked up as it all may seem
The consequences that I've rendered
I've gone and fucked things up again

—Staind

Comfort precedes collapse

—Vance Havner

WHAT THEY DON'T teach you in Narcotics Anonymous is that addiction is cunning and insidious for no reason. If there is any small way for addiction to sneak back into your life, even the slightest crack in the foundation of recovery that you stand upon, it will creep in. I lost sight of the ball. I had put far too much distance between myself and my past, and I had done nothing but focus on building myself up from the outside. I say addiction is insidious because it will not overwhelm you all at once; it will slowly deceive you into believing you can somehow manage to control it.

My backslides rarely ever started with hard drugs. They always began with the most socially accepted drug of all, alcohol. If I had sipped one glass of wine that night, then continued drinking until I got drunk and woke up horribly hungover, I more than likely wouldn' have drank again. I would have recognized immediately I was still the same alcoholic, that nothing had changed, and I couldn't manage it. Instead, my addiction lied to me. It flirted with the inner recess of my mind that felt more comfortable as a failure and lured me into believing I was able to control my drinking.

If I was a functioning drinker, I wouldn't have gone home thinking about the drink I had and obsessing over it the entire next day. I wouldn't have gone on a date the next night and ordered two glasses of wine, but I did. Then on the third day, when I had three glasses of wine, I wouldn't have lost control—but I did. Those three glasses insidiously stole my inhibitions and reason, and instead of going home, I drove across town to a ladies night at a local bar, and the mixed drinks and shots flowed. Suddenly, I was sixteen years old again. As soon as I got drunk, the old me came out. I was no longer a 32-year-old business owner; I was a 16-year-old thug who only cared about two things: taking a woman home, or if that failed, fighting someone. I got nasty and cursed at people and talked to women with complete disrespect if they didn't show immediate interest in me. Then I repeated it each night that followed.

Two days later I was at a fundraiser party hosted by some friends on the rooftop deck of a local bar. There was a DJ, and I alternated between dancing and going back and forth to the bar all night. An off duty cop from another county who was there became belligerently drunk. When the bar closed at the end of the night and people were filtering out, he smacked a girl I knew on the ass.

When I heard her scream at him, I walked over and said, "Yo, what the fuck is wrong with you?"

His face balled up with drunken hatred and he turned to me and said, "Fuck you, bitch!"

I didn't bother responding. I punched him directly in his mouth. His lip burst open, and he stumbled backwards into the stairs and fell down the double flight of steps leading to the lobby below the rooftop deck. As the bouncers rushed to help him, he began trying to fight them too. He was carried out the front door and into the street, and nearby police rushed over. He began to fight them too. He was handcuffed and taken away. The owner of the establishment was a friend of mine. I used to promote parties for him. The bouncers defended me when he asked what happened because they knew me and had seen the guy's actions prior to me punching him. As the police came into the building, the owner took me into the kitchen, handed me a bottle of liquor, and told me to hide out there in the dark until it was safe. The police came through, searching the back of the restaurant with flashlights, and eventually left. This close encounter wasn't nearly enough to stop me.

I carried on drinking for a couple weeks. I received a warning for smacking a guy in front of the police at another local bar. I was usually out running bails until about 10 PM, so I typically didn't start drinking until late, and then closed the bars out. The next morning I would wake up with horrible anxiety and depression coupled with a hangover, and I would obsess over drinking all day long until I finally had a chance to do it again. I tried to be responsible with drinking and driving. I knew any criminal charges could result in me losing my bail bonds license and everything I had worked so hard to build, but even that didn't stop me. One night I went to a local night club and gave a friend my car keys once I got there so I wouldn't drive home drunk. I called up a friend from the city, a Black dude from West Baltimore, who stuck out in Bel Air like a sore thumb, and invited him out with me. I was belligerent and cocky in the club all night, calling women names and threatening their boyfriends. As was customary at this point in time, my bar tab reached a few hundred dollars from buying everyone shots and trying to show off. At the end of the night I didn't have a woman to take home, understandably so. So I decided to argue and pick a fight with my friend to get my car keys back.

My other friend from Baltimore cut in and offered to take me home. Finally, the two of them convinced me to get in his car. He was driving a rental car at the time and was far away from home.

"Stop here!" I said, pointing at the 7-11 convenience store in Bel Air. "They sell liquor until 2 AM. It's the only place around that does."

"You still want more to drink?" he asked, surprised.

"Yeah, just pull in!"

He pulled into the 7-11, and we walked in together. I walked towards the alcohol, and the older woman behind the counter yelled back, "Excuse me, it's after 2:00." Selling alcohol after 2 AM was a violation of state law.

I pleaded with her. When she wouldn't concede and sell me alcohol, I began cursing at her. I walked back to the liquor section with the intent to just grab some and walk out, when my friend intercepted me.

"I'm calling the cops!" she bellowed from behind the register.

He pleaded with her to calm down and assured her that he would get me out of there. Here he was, a Black dude from the city with gold teeth in his mouth, way out of his element in small town Bel Air, pleading with the older White lady to show lenience on me.

She finally relented and told him, "Fine. Just get him outta here!"

He tossed me the keys to the rental car and told me to go wait in the car. I argued a bit, but finally did as he asked, and that is the last thing that I remember.

I awoke the next day around noon face down in my couch, dehydrated and hung over. I instantly scrambled to find my phone. It was nowhere to be found. I pulled apart the couch cushions and frantically searched through my apartment. I couldn't believe I'd been this irresponsible. I probably missed out on a handful of bail bonds phone calls. *How can I possibly own a business where no one answers the phone? And why haven't I heard it vibrating?* I hopped onto the computer and onto social media and messaged a friend and asked them to call my phone. *Nothing. Shit, if I lost it, this will be a huge dilemma.* I pulled all my furniture away from the walls and finally located the phone underneath the couch. It was dead. I quickly plugged it into the wall and sat waiting for a charge. My next problem would be to figure out how to get back to my car so I could process the bails once they called. I waited, tapping my foot impatiently, for the phone to charge up. When it finally came to life, it blew up with voicemails and text messages as they loaded one right after another—almost all of them from my friend from Baltimore the night before.

The text messages were an escalating scale of panic, starting with "yo," and then "where are you?" followed by a "this shit ain't funny," and finally a "what the fuck?" I quickly picked up the phone to dial him, not even bothering to listen to the voice messages.

He picked up on the first ring, "Yo. Where have you been, yo?"

"At my house, I just woke up. What's wrong? What happened?" I replied nonchalantly.

"My fucking rental car. I need that rental car," he said, clearly agitated.

"I don't know where it's at," I replied honestly.

"You stole it! What the fuck you mean you don't know where it is? I'm stranded out here in bumfuck hillbilly-ville and had to catch a cab to a hotel room cause you stole my shit. And you don't know where it is?"

My stomach dropped for a second, but then rationale came back. "I didn't take your car."

"Where you at? You're home, right? Look outside and tell me it's not there."

I walked to the window and slid the curtain open, and my heart sank. *I better get in the frame of mind for a fight*, I thought to myself. *Or maybe I deserve a beating. I can't believe what I've done.* I was grateful he didn't call the police, but I knew better. It would have ruined my life, but thankfully that wasn't even an option in street code.

"So what's the address there?" he asked. I gave it to him, then walked outside to make sure I hadn't done any damage. When I got outside, I found the car to be locked. I searched around the car, then went back into the apartment and tore the place apart a second time searching for the keys. When he pulled up in a cab, I wanted to hide my face. I wanted to disappear off of the face of the Earth, not out of fear but because of shame. When he approached, I explained to him about the keys and handed him $500 in cash.

"I'm sure the keys are inside the car," I told him. "I've searched everywhere. They've got to be inside underneath a seat. This is for the trouble last night and to get the lock opened. It's the least I can do."

"They can't be inside," he replied. "The doors won't lock if the keys are inside the car".

Instinctively, he started walking around looking through the grass, and I followed suit in a different direction.

"You don't think you threw them out do you?" he asked.

"I don't remember anything from last night, bro. I have no idea what I did," I said apologetically.

We both walked over to the dumpster enclosure about 25

feet from the car. There were the keys, laying on the ground a few feet away from the dumpster.

"Bro, you're something else. You need to get help, bro. Seriously." He walked over to the car and drove off.

Apparently during my blackout when he instructed me to wait in the car at 7-11, I hopped in the driver's seat and took off and drove myself home. I was so belligerently drunk when I pulled up in front of my apartment building that I locked the car and tossed the keys towards the dumpster. I then proceeded into my apartment building, unlocked my apartment, walked in, and passed out directly onto the couch. He was right, I did need help. I decided at that point I needed to control my drinking better. I certainly couldn't stop. After all, the hangover combined with the terrible anxiety and depression from my guilt from drinking and my actions while drinking ensured that I needed to drink again to soothe them.

The next few days I went on drinking just enough to get mildly drunk, but not enough to cause trouble. Then one night I found myself in Park Heights in West Baltimore doing bails until late. On the way home I stopped at a fine dining restaurant called *Crush* that I frequented at the time. I ordered dinner and had a couple glasses of wine. There were a couple of women at the bar paying me no attention, so I started texting everyone in my phone looking for plans. I got desperate and texted old friends I hadn't talked to in years.

Finally, one of them replied and said they were at a bar in Bel Air celebrating an old friend, Jimmy's, birthday. This was an old group of friends who were all drunks and fighters, and I had avoided them for years, but now that I was drinking again I imagined it would be a blast reuniting with them. I sped back to Harford County, making the hour drive in about

40 minutes, and strolled into the bar just before closing time. The bar was packed with people dancing. I said hello to my old friends, then made my way to the bar just in time to grab two beers right before last call. I slammed them both frantically and met back up with my old friends and started working the crowd to see what women were there.

I was upset that the bar was soon to close, but they let me know the party was going to continue back at the birthday boy's hotel room in Edgewood. As was customary, as the bar closed and the crowds dispersed into the parking lot, a fight broke out between my group of friends and some other guys. I remember, not proudly, peeing into the open window of one of their cars, and all over their backseat while they traded threats with my friends in the parking lot. The bouncers poured into the parking lot and broke everything up before it got physical, and we dispersed in separate cars.

Before heading back to the hotel, I started dialing numbers in my phone like crazy. I managed to get ahold of an attractive girl I'd been courting and convinced her to come to the hotel with me. Then I contacted my friend who owned a bar and convinced him to sell me a bottle of liquor. I picked her up, then pulled up around the back of the bar, grabbed the bottle of liquor, and headed to the hotel. The scene at the Ramada Inn was like an old reunion. The same cast of characters I had begun my drinking career with almost two decades earlier were all there. The difference was that while they were still living the exact same way, I had changed completely. Well, I had changed up until these last two weeks. I had an air of confidence and cockiness that I never had before. Instead of being the smallest in the room, I was now the largest. And instead of not having a female with me, I now had the prettiest.

Within a couple hours, everyone had filtered out of the hotel room to go home except for me and my girl and the birthday boy and his. The birthday boy, like me, was a mean drunk, but worse. I never took my aggression out on women. He, however, was known to beat up on women. He tried to hit on the girl I had brought with me in front of his girlfriend all night long. He was extremely jealous, and by the end of the night he started beating on his girlfriend right in front of us. He punched her and spit on her face. I couldn't take it anymore.

"Why don't you chill the fuck out?" I stood up.

He puffed up back at me with a drunken glare in his eyes, "Why don't you make me, bitch?"

The rest was a blur.

We somehow ended up on the second-floor landing outside of the front door of the hotel room, he was sprawled out on the ground, and I had his blood all over me. The cops showed up almost instantly. As the police finished walking the stairs to the landing, Jimmy, drunk and dazed had just finished climbing to his feet. They recognized him almost instantly. The police were there for a noise complaint. Once they saw who had gotten beaten up, they didn't even care about the fight.

"Oh, I'm sure he deserved it," one of them laughed.

"When are you going to get your shit together, Jimmy?" Another one teased. They all traded mild insults with each other.

Jimmy talked shit back, and then they got serious.

"Look, we're not going to arrest anybody, but you guys need to break this up. So anyone who's not sleeping here needs to go. We'll call you a cab because you certainly aren't driving."

My girl and I obliged, and moments later when the cab arrived, we hopped in. The police pulled away as we pulled off, and we began a discussion with the cab driver about where to take us. Then my heart skipped a beat.

"Shit! My phone is in that hotel room! I need you to go back!" I said to the cab driver. This started an argument back and forth with the cab driver about whether to go back or not because the police had instructed him to take us away from the hotel. After several moments, I won. The cabbie circled around back into the Ramada Inn, and I ran up to the second floor and began beating on the door. Nobody answered.

"I just need my phone. My phone is in there!" I yelled to the closed door. I beat my fist even louder on the door while the cab driver and horrified young lady both watched and waited below. Within moments the police returned, and I was handcuffed, arrested, and taken to jail for trespassing.

It had been about a decade since I had been inside of a detention center as a criminal. I had come in a professional capacity here every day for years to post bails with the commissioner. I had made friends with all of the commissioners. They knew my story of overcoming my past and how far I had come. We talked about our families, our accomplishments, our lives. Yet, here I was waiting to see a commissioner at 3 AM, blackout drunk and covered in someone else's blood because I had just assaulted them. This time my visit was to be on the other side of the glass.

I don't remember much of my visit, but I know even in my drunken state of mind I was ashamed. Like a puppy with his tail between his legs, I sat on the other side of the glass partition that separates the inmates from the district court commissioner. The young lady across from me just shook her head at me. What had become of me? This young man whom she had befriended and done business with every day.

She knew this was not me, at least not the real me. She held my hearing, and because trespassing is a petty charge, I was released that night. I got home and went to sleep as the sun was coming up. And when I awoke, I never touched another drop of alcohol again. That was May 21, 2011.

My recovery and personal evolution took a major change starting that next day. I began chasing the sun. I dabbled back in meetings, took on a sponsor, and began to work the steps. And I started going back to church. I still worked like crazy, but my focus was on personal growth instead of chasing women and building up my outside image. I began to read books again, not novels, but spiritual growth books such as *The Alchemist* by Paul Coehlo and *The Four Agreements* by Don Miguel Ruiz. A slow but sudden shift was happening inside of me. After ten years of mostly recovery, I was finally re-realizing that there was a deeper sense of purpose to my life than chasing after the worldly success I had never before achieved. I had, after all, finally attained a material status I never imagined possible for myself. Now, it was time to show my gratitude and start figuring out why I was still alive. It was time for me to live this life that I didn't feel I deserved.

I had been on many spiritual pilgrimages like this before, where I had delved into world religions, and self-study. However, those missions were often clouded by the smokescreen of drugs and alcohol, or were hindered by the fact that I had no outside freedom. It is hard to take time to look inside yourself and learn about yourself when the pressures of the world are upon you. I couldn't exactly find true freedom in personal exploration when I wasn't sure how I was going to feed and shelter myself, or pay bills, or even get out from the heavy pressure from my parents to move out into the world. Now it was time. All of the events of my previous 32 years on earth had led me here, and somehow they hadn't killed me. It was time I start showing my Creator some gratitude. And that's what I set out to do...

Then it happened again. About a month after my drinking incident ended, one morning I awoke at 4 AM, alone in my apartment, cold, and yet my skin flushed hot and tingled. The world zeroed in on me in that ungodly hour, and for no reason at all terror struck every nerve in my body at once. I shook and I cried. Panic rocked me in waves. Life seemed all at once purposeless, and my very existence had no meaning. I tried to lay back in bed, but my heart palpitated. I begged God to rescue me, and when He didn't, I begged him to take me away from this planet.

My anxiety was back full force, and mixed so forcefully with my depression that a master bartender couldn't mix together a stronger cocktail. I bided three hours of inner torture and extreme panic on my couch until the sun started to rise and I knew the world would be awakening. All I could think was, "I need my mother." I just needed someone I could trust to be around. I knew from previous episodes that this would last about two weeks and I wouldn't be able to function through it. There was nowhere I could go and nothing I could do to make it stop. The only thing that seemed to make me feel the least bit safe was being around those I loved and trusted. At 7 AM my mother received a phone call.

I was sobbing on the other end, "Mom, I need to come over. It's happening again. I'm freaking out, terrified. I don't know what to do."

Thirty-three years old, a successful bail bondsman, weightlifter, player, money chaser, Mr. Tough Guy was broken and terrified and calling his mommy to rescue him from himself. There were no other women to run to this time. I was all alone and scared to death of myself. I got in the car and somehow drove to my parents' house and shadowed them through the coming days, sleeping in their spare bedroom until the panic began to subside little by little. The mornings were always the worst. I would awake at an extremely early hour, stricken with intense anxiety and depression, and I'd wait alone for the rest of the world to awaken from their slumber. Throughout the day, anxiety would deplete so much energy from my body that I would begin to feel depleted enough to cause the panic to subside.

My mother made a comment in passing that forever changed the trajectory of my life: "If you're not ready to go back to work yet, why don't you do something with yourself during the day that might make you feel better? They are doing a soup kitchen at the church tomorrow, and they could use your help."

As simple as it sounds, the very thought of doing anything was terrifying. Laying around all day praying for grace or even death while suffering this inner torment was terrifying, but so was the idea of taking on any kind of task. "I don't think I can," I whined. It was embarrassing to admit, even to my own mother. I couldn't do anything or take on anything except my inner invisible demons. I could neither conquer nor escape them.

Her simple response, "Why can't you?" was a hard one to argue with.

I arrived at the church and tried to stay in the back kitchen cutting vegetables and washing dishes. My head played games with me the whole time, but as long as I stayed busy, I could win the battle. I did my best. It was a simple task, and yet I focused on every task like I was trying to win a prize at it. I washed dishes by hand at a speed and with a thoroughness that I hoped would impress others. I chopped vegetables quickly and trayed them and then begged for more work. I was in a zone, and when the homeless arrived to eat, I stepped way out of my comfort zone.

I walked out into that auditorium where all the tables had been set and arranged, and I took in all of the crowds of people there, half of them homeless and the other half servants. I justified in my mind that these were my people. I was a freak. I was a freak inside of my mind, and if there was anyone who wouldn't judge me, it would be the homeless who I was about to serve. I had been one of them many times myself, and many of them, if not most, had their own inner demons in the form of mental illness. The only difference between me and them was that I had somehow gotten a few worldly possessions and no longer slept on the street. My Cadillac Escalade, my designer clothes, jewelry, apartment, and business were all just a very thin line that separated me from them. In fact it was all an illusion, we weren't separate at all.

I grabbed some trays of food and delivered them to people who were seated waiting for their meal. I ran around breaking a sweat while delivering plates, greeting the people with kind words and smiles. I wanted to use the energy that was eating me alive to somehow make them feel better. I refilled drinks and took away dirty plates and happily brought seconds to those who were still hungry. It became an honor for me to serve them. I felt almost unworthy to be there that day fulfilling such a meager and yet important role. These were kings and queens, and I was but a mere servant who God placed there that day, and when I stepped into that role, my anxiety dissipated.

When I left that day and got into my truck to drive home, the sun had broken through the cold March clouds, and I felt the very first sign that spring was on its way. I was going to be alright. As usual, I was going to be more than alright, and life was going to be normal again. Maybe even…it would be good.

I found a new high. It wasn't a high that was self-destructive, and it certainly wasn't going to take over my life. It was a feel-good drug that was mild and non-addictive. Instead of being fueling my ego and myself, it was quite the opposite. This new 'drug' was purpose, and its side effect was service. I began serving the homeless community in shelters and soup kitchens and delivering groceries around the county to people in need much like I had done with my parents in my youth. Only this time, no one was forcing me to do it. The more I began to serve those less fortunate than me, the more my eyes began to open. Between the service work, the self-studies, and the twelve steps, my mind began to blossom more and more. New realizations, that I had been intentionally blind to, began to flourish within me.

I no longer lived in a self-absorbed bubble, and I began to look for opportunities to help and to fulfill my purpose. The notion of fulfilling one's purpose is sometimes thought to be self-absorbed and ego fulfilling, but this was a much more pure notion. There was also a selfish notion that I wanted, or even had to do things, to keep the inner anxiety away. I began to believe that the more purely I lived and the more I surrendered to God's will and served this planet and the people on it, the less likely it was that my anxiety would return. This became a large catalyst for everything I did from that moment forward. Whether true or not, it was a necessary sacrifice I was willing to make in order to keep those terrifying episodes at bay. I would do anything not to face those dark times ever again. It is in this strange irony that I have chosen to look at my anxiety and depression as a gift. If I ever even consider the idea of straying off course, it is the very thought of my panic attacks returning that keeps me in check. It is my anxiety that serves as a backup plan to keep me on the righteous path, to keep me honest, and to keep me in servitude, gratitude, and humility. My anxiety will never let me cheat on a spouse, sell drugs, steal, lie, or hurt anyone. My anxiety ultimately humbled me and brought me closer to God, much like heroin had done over a decade before. My biggest curse became my greatest blessing. When it comes, it comes hard and makes me wish for death, but I hold on tight through it because I know it has brought me through so many levels of personal evolution that I would never have gotten this far without it.

My life began to revolve around inner exploration rather than exterior matters such as materials and financial obsession. My bail bonds company had grown to a place where I had several full-time employees, so I wasn't on call around the clock anymore. I was willing to invest money into hiring people in order to give myself some personal freedom. My physical health became a priority again, and I started losing weight and toning up by making it to the gym regularly. I continued looking for ways to build not only my business, but also my spiritual portfolio. I tried new things like skydiving, massages, and yoga. A yoga studio opened up down the street, and I wandered in and grabbed a schedule of classes. I had always been intrigued by all things spiritual, no matter their source or culture. I had studied Buddhism, Hinduism, the Tao, ancient Egyptian spiritual practices, etc. Yoga wasn't trendy yet, and was a fairly new concept in our area, so it caught my attention. When I finally had enough nerve, I wandered in for a beginner class one evening.

I got a loaner mat and nervously laid it out in the back of the room so nobody could see me fumble through the movements. I was still extremely shy and nervous and entirely out of my element. We began with a light meditation. My mind raced the whole time. Then we went into beginning stretches. These were very basic movements, but like usual in life, I pushed myself past the point of comfortability and deep into the stretches. I exhausted myself way too early for what was to come. This was a beginner class, yet I couldn't keep up. I was the only male in a room of about twenty women, and I was also the youngest. By all appearances I was also the most fit person in the room, but looks can be deceiving. As this room full of middle-aged women gracefully transitioned between movements, I sweat profusely and shook the whole time. I often stopped to kneel on the sweaty mat with my head on the floor taking 'child's pose' just hoping the class was almost over. It seemed to stretch on for eternity. Finally in a great moment of reprieve, the teacher asked us to get comfortable on our mats, and she led us through a longer guided meditation.

She told us to envision a special, happy place. My mind immediately went to where I spent my summers as a child at my grandparents' RV trailer on the eastern shore of the Chesapeake Bay at a campground called Cherrystone. It was my favorite place on earth growing up, and my grandmother loved me like no other. I eventually got kicked out of the campground in my teenage years for criminal behavior and wasn't allowed back for over a decade. But as I lay there on that mat, my mind drifted off to the campsite and the bay stretched out in front of me. The tall pine trees, the wind drifting through the reeds as the summer sun set on the horizon, the smell of campfire smoke, my whole family together, the dreaminess of a young boy just learning the world. My grandmother was no longer alive, but her warm smile came in and out of my mind as I lay there on that mat envisioning the paradise of my youth and tears spilled down my cheeks onto the mat below. I let them spill out in waves. I didn't care who saw them, I was proud of them.

When the teacher roused us out of meditation and asked us to sit up for a final affirmation, I brought myself up to my knees, and rested in cross-legged pose with red eyes and wet cheeks. I didn't even bother to wipe them. I wasn't ashamed of where my mind had taken me; I wanted to go back forever. But life is tragically beautiful and always changing. I had to find my new happy place. I would hunt for it, and I would chase that sun over the horizon and beyond.

The brisk fall air felt refreshing on my sweat-soaked body as I walked to my car, not sure what could possibly be worth doing for the rest of the evening after that experience. I was told yoga opens the body through a series of deep stretches. Through stretching parts of the body that we are unaccustomed to stretching, we are opening much needed gateways within our body. Further, the philosophy of 'as above, so below' is found to permeate much of eastern religion and philosophy. Yoga embraces this by opening the closed-off parts of the body, we also open untapped parts of the mind. I sat in my car for a while after class, then I drove out of the parking lot and pulled over two blocks away into a convenience store parking lot. I sat there, cool, refreshed, and for lack of a better word, open. I had never felt so open. I sat there basking in this amazing feeling, and my mind danced in all different directions. I'm not sure what line of thought brought me to this point, but I was secure in the realization that I needed to do more. I had given some of my time to serving the community, but I hadn't given any of my money. I was doing well financially. In fact, I was doing better than I had ever dreamed or deserved to be doing. It was time that I give back.

It was now the winter of 2011, Christmas was around the corner, and that was an obvious answer to me. I could help people out for Christmas. *What people, though? And where will I find these people?* Then I thought of my past and my current bail bonds business, and it all started to fit together like pieces of a puzzle. *What if I made a list of all the children who had lost parents to addiction, or whose parents were incarcerated due to addiction, and buy them Christmas gifts?* Children shouldn't have to suffer for their parents choices or addictions, and I surely didn't want them to miss out on Christmas because of it. Besides, the less these children felt like outcasts, maybe just maybe, the less likely they would be to repeat the same choices their parents had. I wanted to make these children feel special for Christmas with the little I had to give. I picked the amount of $2,500 out of thin air and figured I could take 50 children shopping for $50 worth of gifts each for Christmas. It was a small gesture, but a worthy one, and it proved to be the start of something much, much bigger.

I took to social media to promote the upcoming Toy Run and sent fliers out to community centers and jails. Soon, my phone was blowing up with people in need of help. I began a vetting process to make sure these were legitimate cases. Not all the children came from families who suffered because of addiction. Some were other cases of hardship, but I couldn't say no. A few people saw what I was doing on social media and volunteered to help. A week before Christmas we met 60 children and their guardians at a local Toys-R-Us and let them shop while we waited at the register to pay for everything as they checked out. The smiles, gratitude, and hugs from children were more than I ever expected. I never expected to get so much gratitude for something so small. I was a single man with no children. Giving $3,000 when I was making six figures was a relatively small thing, and yet it was huge. It was huge considering that a decade ago I was stealing and robbing everyone I came in contact with just to get my next high. I was banned from stores all across the state, and yet here I was connecting with management to arrange a toy run to give away thousands to help others.

I took to social media to share the glory and to thank people who supported the effort. There were tons of pictures of me with smiling children. Sometimes I look back and cringe at how many pictures I was in. I still wrestled with my ego early on; I wanted to be seen. My posts caught a lot of attention and a lot of congratulations, but most importantly they inspired others to get involved. This was key. There were always some who would condemn me for showing what I'd done, claiming I was bragging. Maybe there was some bragging involved, but more than that, for me, there was a lot of proof—proof that one guy like me could make a big impact. Sharing it on social media also laid the groundwork for even greater efforts in the future. If it wasn't for those posts on social media, my charity work wouldn't have blossomed the way it did. The Toy Run grew year by year until we were taking 250 children shopping for Christmas, and the local news stations were there broadcasting it.

In the Gospel of Matthew, Jesus says, "Nor do they light a lamp and then put it under a bushel basket; it is set on a lamp stand, where it gives light to all in the house. Just so, your light must shine before others, that they may see your good deeds and glorify your heavenly Father." I began to realize I could be a light for others. By sharing my story and my actions, I could inspire those who were walking down the path of hopelessness I once walked. I quickly gained a following of people who were just like I once was, and they wanted to give back and make an impact. My charity work quickly grew into more projects that involved working with homeless, and children, and senior citizens in need. I became a household name, but this time it wasn't for my crazy behavior or for promoting nightclubs. It wasn't even for bail bonds. It was for something much more fulfilling. As a result, my self-image and my belief in myself grew at an incredible pace.

My eyes were opened to a new world of possibilities. The more I believed in myself and my potential, the more I began to explore what this world had to offer. I was single and had decided to take to the internet to search for yoga retreats in different countries. I found one in Tulum, Mexico called Maya Tulum. The funny thing is that when I got there, I didn't do any yoga. However, I did tons of learning and self-exploration. I flew to Mexico by myself and caught a bus for a two-hour ride south of Cancun to a waterfront resort. Tulum is an eco-tourism town. It is a natural and beautiful mecca for hippies and spiritual seekers from all over the world. There are no high-rises or huge hotels, instead it consists of a long road along the Caribbean Sea littered with eclectic beach front hotels, most of which do not have TVs in the rooms, or even electricity for that matter. It is a haven for yoga enthusiasts, new age spiritual seekers, naturalists, and beach goers alike. The Mayan jungle comes all the way up to the edge of the long white sand beach that stretches for miles along the blue ocean.

One balmy Saturday, I checked in and was guided through a series of sandy pathways on the way to my own personal hut just off of the beach about twelve feet from the ocean waves. Inside the thatch roofed hut was a bed, a desk, and a bathroom. This was my home for the week, and I had never been so excited. In the mornings I would sit on the step of my hut and drink coffee and do crosswords and watch the pelicans circle and dive for fish. Then I would walk a mile or two in the hot sun along the sandy beach enjoying the views of topless women sunbathing, the Mayan-themed architecture of each hotel, and of course the natural beauty all around me. Some days I would lay on the beach and read or walk into town to try lunch at a local restaurant and go shopping. Other days I would take guided tours of Mayan ruins or an excursion to snorkel or swim in an underground river. Every night after dinner, I would book a spa experience, whether it be a Thai massage, or a Mayan clay massage, or a sound wave experience with crystals and essential oils. Then I would wander in the starry night back to my hut on the water and read until I fell asleep. I was worlds away from Baltimore City and the draining lifestyle of being in bail bonds and dealing with pain and deceit every day. Most importantly, I spent time with myself away from all distractions, and I discovered I actually enjoyed my own company. I loved being alone in nature. For the first time in my life, I no longer had to run from myself. I didn't need to stay busy to avoid myself, and I certainly didn't need alcohol or drugs to escape who I was anymore. I came back to Tulum by myself every Valentine's Day for a few years, even when I was in a relationship. It was a part of me now.

I wasn't a street junkie anymore. I was a travel junkie now. A friend of mine who liked to surf had talked for years about how he was going to quit his job and move to Costa Rica to bartend and surf down there for the rest of his life. After hearing his talk for a long time, he finally announced that he was going and that he'd secured a place for six months. His goal was to use those six months to explore, find a job, and secure permanent housing. He then extended an invitation to me and assured me that I had a free place to stay should I ever want to come down.

Three weeks later, I was on a plane by myself flying into Liberia, Costa Rica. He told me when I exited the airport to just ask a taxi driver to take me to the town of Villareal. I hopped into a cab and told him where to take me. He shrugged his shoulders. *Great, he doesn't understand English.* He got out and consorted with some other taxi drivers. They all approached me, and after a few minutes it was obvious they had no idea where Villareal was. I started getting nervous, so I called my friend Phil and explained the situation.

"Look, it's about an hour drive. Just tell them to take you to Tamarindo. I'll go out onto the highway in 45 minutes. Just look for me at the bus stops."

I turned to the cabbie and said, "Tamarindo," and his eyes lit up. We were on our way.

Scorched Earth. That's the only way I know how to explain

my first impression of Costa Rica. The first thirty minutes of our drive was through fields of dried yellow and brown grasses. Everything was dead, and the sun was shining down on us at 100 degrees or better. It was dry season in Costa Rica, and hadn't rained a drop in three months. The dry season would carry on for another three months, into the month of May, before it would rain for almost six months straight. But now, everything looked bleak and destitute besides the bright sun, all something I would come to love and embrace.

The cab driver and I joked in our mixed languages, and he blared Michael Jackson out of the speakers. I pulled out a cigar, and he asked excitedly and through a sly grin if it was marijuana. He also offered to stop at a store so I could buy *cervezas*. To his disappointment I told him no drugs or drinks for me. The further we drove into this foreign country, the more I got nervous. I was in the middle of nowhere. There were no hotels, no fast food restaurants, and what I did see looked dingy and run-down. Everything was intimidating and foreign to me. Little did I know within a couple of years this would all become familiar and natural to me.

About an hour into our drive, and making our way over a couple of mountains, the scenery around us started getting greener, and I began seeing signs advertising surf shops and restaurants. We came to a small town, and there was my buddy Phil standing on the corner with a surfboard with a big smile on his face. *Thank God.* I urged the cab driver to pull over immediately. I hopped out, grabbed my suitcase, paid the driver, and Phil and I were on our way. I dragged my suitcase in the dirt behind me for about a quarter mile along the road, then we turned off into the woods and down a dirty driveway to Phil's home.

"Go ahead and get unpacked and get ready. We're going to head out to the Crazy Monkey soon. That's the big Friday night spot in town."

Phil was a drinker. He liked to bartend and party, but he knew where I stood. He also informed me that there was a female was staying with us, but she had disappeared on a coke binge for a few days with a couple of locals. Apparently, this friend of his had a problem with cocaine and had come down to Costa Rica to dry out. They had an understanding that she could come as long as there were no hard drugs involved. That had backfired rather quickly. *What have I gotten myself into?*

We got dressed and caught a ten-minute cab ride into town. As we went down the hill from Villareal to Tamarindo, it began to look more like paradise. Palm trees appeared. An estuary on the left side of the road emptied out into the Pacific Ocean that lay ahead of us. And stores and restaurants lined both sides of the street. People were everywhere. Beautiful people: white, brown, and black. Some were shirtless and carrying surfboards, and others were dressed up for a night on the town of fine dining or dancing.

We pulled up to the beach and gave the cabbie two dollars and hopped out. Phil informed me that dinner would be chicken skewers that someone was cooking on a grill on the side of the road. We bought a couple and scarfed them down. They were amazing. Then we hiked up the long set of stairs into the Crazy Monkey. At the top of the stairs, security was collecting a five-dollar cover. We paid and walked in. The place was huge, all open air with several rooms and no walls. There was a hip hop area around a pool, a room with cocktail bars and house music, and a room with salsa dancing in the back. There were easily a few hundred people here. What especially caught my eye were the tons of brown and black skinned women in heels and skirts who were absolutely stunning and all looking straight at me. I felt like a piece of fresh meat walking into a lion's den. I was clean cut, muscular, and obviously new here. My ego told me immediately that they were all attracted to me.

Phil went to the bar and grabbed me a cranberry juice and two beers for himself, and we sat at a table catching up. His female roommate was supposed to meet us here, and as time ticked on I could sense his frustration when she didn't show. He told me disgustedly about how her trip down was supposed to go, and how he assumed that instead she was out having sex with tourists and locals for coke. I half listened and sympathized with him as my eyes scanned the room. Absolutely gorgeous women all around the bar played eye contact games with me and made obvious flirtatious smiles at me while Phil and I talked. Finally, I said to him, "Phil, what is it with this place? These women are on me. They won't stop flirting."

He laughed. "The only words they know how to say in English are '100 dollars.'"

"You don't understand. They are looking at me way different than that." My ego was in control now. "Look at that one over at the bar. She won't stop. She definitely likes me."

The two women from the bar came walking over. The one who had been eyeing me up since I walked in hung slightly back. The other one approached me, leaned into my ear and said, "Hey, my friend really likes you."

"Well, I really like her too," I replied looking her up and down. I looked over at Phil as if to say, "I told you so."

He just smiled, a knowing smile.

I tried to communicate directly, but it seemed as if her beautiful friend didn't speak English. As if on cue, Phil rose to his feet and said, "Well, I'm going to head back to the house. Do you want to come with me or stay here?"

I was trapped.

The young lady whispered in my ear, "You should stay here. My friend really thinks you are sexy."

Finally, I caved and decided to throw all caution to the wind. "How much does she want?"

"She wants to be your girlfriend. Do you have $100?"

I looked over at Phil.

His smirk said, "I told you so."

I was nervous, but I was also single, in a foreign country, and had a wad of $100 bills in my pocket. *Why not?* I bid him farewell. The young lady who had hung slightly back now stepped forward and smiled deeply with warm eyes as if she was in love with me, and she took my hand. We walked together hand in hand out of the club, and I felt like a prince. She said hello to the many people passing by that she knew and then said goodbye to her friends at security as we descended the staircase to leave. It reminded me of many decades before when I had lost my virginity to the girl at Cherrystone…the way she walked me around hand in hand as if I were some sort of prize she had won, and not vice versa.

We walked the street in the dark, passing drunk tourists and locals who gawked at her beauty and even made comments in Spanish that I couldn't understand. Then we turned left up an alleyway and approached a metal gate. She spoke to a guard in a small shack next to the gate and handed him money in the dark, and he exited and opened the gate for us. There was a small, dingy courtyard beyond lined with doors, reminiscent of a Costa Rican version of a roadside motel. She led me to one of the doors and opened it, and I followed her inside, full of trepidation. As she clicked on the lights, they buzzed and flickered brightly into the room. There was nothing but a bed and a bathroom. Bugs scurried across the floor in the luminescent light, and it almost reminded me of a prison cell. I walked nervously into the bathroom to take a piss then came out to meet her standing next to the bed. She put one hand on each of my shoulders and gracefully pushed me down to sit on the bed in front of her. Reaching into her purse, she got a condom and set it next to me on the bed. Her innocence and beauty were such a contradiction to this dank room and what was taking place inside of it. I was leery and squirming inside.

As she began to undress before me in her charming, seductive manner, I just wanted to talk to her. I wanted to talk to her and tell her she deserved more than this, but I couldn't. We had a language barrier. I looked her in her eyes, visually pleading for her to understand who I was. I wasn't like her usual clients. I didn't want to hurt her. I didn't want to use her. I wanted better for her. I simply couldn't go through with this. She was human just like me. I stood up and embraced her and pulled her half-removed shirt back down over her body. I reached into my pocket and handed her $100 and quietly said, "Gracias," thanking her again. I wanted her to understand I wasn't ending things because I was unattracted to her. It was deeper. Coming here with her, I was trying to be someone that I wasn't, and it didn't work. I felt like she understood immediately. She took my hand and walked me back out of the courtyard to the street and kissed me on the cheek. I waved a cab back to the house, feeling good about what I had just done. That may have been the easiest $100 she'd make all season. I apparently wasn't what I'd come to think a normal man was. I couldn't just lay down with a stranger and get turned on by it, especially if that experience was a business transaction.

Tamarindo was a tourist town commonly referred to as "Tama-gringo." It was one of the most populated beach towns in Costa Rica and a melting pot of people from all over the world. My buddy Phil did his own thing and surfed most days while I explored and met all kinds of unique people and hung out on the beaches by myself or dined and shopped by myself. I loved it there. My soul felt at home. The only downfall was that on every corner of town, either locals or Colombians would approach me and say, "Hey amigo, what do you need?" And they would proceed to offer me weed, cocaine, or any other assortment of drugs. I got tired of saying no to the same faces day in and day out, even while lying on the beach. Otherwise, it was free and warm, and somewhere I could see myself living out the rest of my days. I explored all of the local cuisine, yoga studios, and massage places. Then at night I would meet up with Phil and his roommate, who had eventually returned, and we would all hang in the bars while they drank. As it got late, I would usually hail a cab back to the house and read while they continued to party. Then while they slept off their hangovers in the mornings, I would head into town and hit the beach.

My seven-day vacation was coming to an end, and I called the airline to extend it for three more days. When the full ten days were over, I boarded a bus back to the airport with tears in my eyes. I didn't want to leave this place and the new friends I had made in town. There was nothing for me at home. I returned to Baltimore extremely depressed for two full days in frigid, late January. On the third day I pulled up to the gym as it was just starting to snow. Sitting in my car before I went inside, I opened my phone and booked flights to Costa Rica for the next morning.

I spent another seven days in Costa Rica much like the first and made friends with locals who would become my friends for life. In the short time I was gone, Phil had flipped his surfboard while surfing one morning, and the fin had gone through his leg. He had been carried out of town by some locals and delivered to a local hospital where he got 45 staples in his leg and a pair of crutches to traverse town. He and his roommate had begun fighting badly, and he was miserable. He spoke of Costa Rica as his own personal hell and vowed that once he returned to the US he would never come back. I, however, was in love. It had quickly become my second home. To this day, I have been back to Costa Rica over 40 times, visiting all different parts of the country, and half of my trips were alone.

The following spring, someone reached out to me and nominated me to run for the Leukemia & Lymphoma Society Man of the Year. I had no personal experience with Leukemia or Lymphoma, nor did I truly understand what it even was. What I did know was, it was a disease, and that this was another chance for me to do something good. I gratefully accepted. My belief was that anything that was brought to me was done so by fate, and therefore I had no choice but to willingly oblige. The Man and Woman of the Year contest, hosted by the LLS, is an annual fundraising event in which they choose several well-known men and women from the community to compete to see who can raise the most money for their cause. Subsequently, whoever did so was chosen as the Man and Woman of the Year. It was an ingenious way to play upon the human ego and spirit of competition in order to raise large amounts of money for a worthy cause. When it came to ego, they found the right person when they chose me. I committed and took it upon myself to go at this new contest without restraint. I dove into it like I dive into any undertaking, with everything that I had.

I became obsessed with raising enough money to earn the Man of the Year title. And though I was up against some more worthy and well-established businessmen in the community, I didn't let that hinder me. I went at it all day every day. I formed a team of people willing to help me and hosted tons of events and fundraisers throughout the spring. I did extremely well and got caught up in the whirlwind of my own egotistical drive to be the best. I was told by some that I had no chance, especially against one of the other contenders who was a well-known mega-real estate agent in the area. Not only that, but he was friends with several members of the LLS Committee. Telling me I couldn't win and that I stood no chance was fuel for me to push even harder. It was almost like that doctor telling me that I could never get clean without methadone and how I walked out of his office and never looked back.

I kept tabs on my numbers with women on the board who I had become close with, and I was in the lead. One of them came to me as the final gala approached in which the winner would be announced.

She said, "Danny, what you've done is amazing, and I don't want you to forget that. But I want you to know that you're not going to win. The game is rigged in his favor."

People had insinuated this to me many times before, but to hear it from her was heartbreaking. Apparently, the LLS held an annual bull roast every year and usually raised several tens of thousands of dollars. At this particular year's event, they raised $40,000 and donated it all to my opponent's campaign, giving him an entirely unfair advantage. Of course, it shouldn't matter in a charity event because we were all competing for the same good cause, and the goal was to raise money to save lives. However, this game designed to play very intensely on the human ego, so I couldn't let his unfair advantage stop me. I continued moving at full force, doing everything I could to raise as much money as possible. Most of my donations came from small people like me in the amounts of $25 or $50. I got a couple of large donations from friends who owned businesses, including a ten-thousand-dollar donation from the insurance company that handled my bail bonds. But for the most part, I was getting money from average street people looking to make a difference, and they did.

At the final gala they called my name, and I walked to the stage through heavy applause dressed in a tuxedo. They announced that I had broken an all-time record by raising $90,000 myself. Then, they announced that my main opponent had raised $94,000, and was therefore granted the Man of the Year title. The room spun around me, and I felt nauseous. I had broken records, and yet coincidentally, so had he. He raised just $4,000 more than me. If he hadn't been given the proceeds from the bull roast, which he shouldn't have been given, then I would have rightfully won the title. I was enraged. One of the men on the board, who was good friends with my opponent, put his hand on my shoulder to congratulate me.

"Don't fucking touch me, you piece of shit," I spat at him. I was sick. I felt the life being sucked out of my body as I walked back to my seat, shaking. My whole table of friends and family knew what had happened. They were angry and upset, but there was nothing anyone could do. I had failed and come in second place as usual, and by unfair means. It was always the story of my life.

Nobody could console me. I was depressed for a few weeks. I had temporarily lost faith in humanity and morality. To an outsider, it was so silly and trivial, but to me it was everything at the time. I had once again received the message that no matter how hard I worked or how deeply I committed myself, I would never be good enough. I lost sight of everything that truly mattered about the event and became consumed by my own ego. I wasn't meant to win. I was never meant to win. Winning would never have strengthened me and given me a struggle through which to grow and learn. The fact of the matter remained: I raised an incredible amount of money for a good cause, and no title I could have received would have filled the hole inside of me. Only my own personal evolution could achieve that. My ridiculous pain eventually brought me closer to God. I was still learning who I was and how to cope with myself. The whole Man of the Year experience was one more lesson in taming my fragile ego.

LEVEL EIGHT

A little smoke, get a little drink,
Kept my head bad, so I couldn't think
Love came along late one night
And I finally see the light
And I'm a changed man.

—The Impressions

THE WHOLE 2011 Man of the Year ordeal had not only established my name further in the philanthropy community, but it introduced me to a lot of like-minded people around Baltimore. I began hanging out and doing service projects and Bible studies with people I had connected with through the fundraising process. So, when a group of them decided they wanted to put together a mission trip to Peru, I eagerly jumped on board. This would bring two of my passions together: service and exploring the world.

Sixteen of us made the mission trip to Peru. The plan was to fly into Lima, then catch another short plane ride to Pucallpa, followed by a boat ride into the Amazon to stay with the Shipibo tribe. Four of us decided we wanted to see Machu Picchu first, so we flew into Peru a week early in order to explore before meeting up with the group for our mission work.

I could write a whole book about my trip to Peru. It is truly a magical country. From snowcapped mountains, to steamy hot jungles, this country has a little bit of everything. I toured ancient ruins, lost cities, alpaca farms, walked through foreign villages alone at night, and wrestled with altitude sickness. We ate alpaca steaks, visited Incan sacrificial altars, browsed crystals at the markets, and hiked Montaña Machu Picchu. A mystical aura was palpable in the air in those Incan mountains.

It's something I'd never forget, and I'd long to return to for years to come.

Our small group returned to Lima to meet with our group then transferred to Pucallpa. It was entirely different country. Instead of cool air and mountains, we were now in the intense heat of the Amazon. We boarded a houseboat that was to be our home for the following week and headed up the Ucayali River several hours deep into the Amazon jungle. Pink dolphins splashed and surfaced in the water around us as we traveled into a region that was so far away from humanity, it felt like a foreign planet. For eight hours we headed up the river into the nether regions of the Amazon, and at nightfall we pulled up to a muddy river bank. We walked out onto the bow of the boat and saw lights flickering at the top of the embankment and voices singing in a strange language in the darkness above.

Glowing faces began to appear, each one looking down on us and waving. We nervously waved back at our hosts for the week. One by one we stepped off of the boat and walked the wood planks onto the muddy embankment. Warm brown hands reached down to us and guide us to the top. They embraced our hands tightly and welcomed us into their circle. They continued singing happily and beautifully in their native Quechua language, moving in a circular motion as the last of the guests joined in. The women were all clothed in handmade dresses that were created for special occasions such as these. We could tell that they respected and appreciated their new guests. It was the warmest welcome I had ever received and one that I will never forget.

One by one the woman of the village broke off from the circle and took us hand in hand into the dark jungle. We had no choice but to trust our new guides. They led us into a large wooden structure that I would soon learn was their church built by previous missionaries. As we sat on the wooden benches, children giggled, pointed, and climbed all over us while we watched the tribespeople sing and perform and welcome us to their community. We then returned to the boat to sleep for the night. The interior rooms of the boat were locked and caged with prison-style bars. This, I would later learn, was to protect us from pirates. Two security guards armed with rifles would sit atop of the boat watching for Amazon pirates during the night. On two separate evenings we heard gunshots and later learned they were warning shots to scare away approaching pirates.

The week went by fast as we built and painted a community center in their village. We also installed water filtration systems in a couple of their meager homes. The heat was intense, the labor was hard, and the bugs were ferocious. However, the experience was dreamy, and the Shipibo people were hospitable. They became our friends in spite of cultural differences and language barriers. The children were amazing, and I noticed that despite having almost nothing of material value, they were kind to one another and appreciative. If one child hurt themselves, the others tended to them. If one child went without a piece of candy, then the others shared. Most miraculously, during the entire week surrounded by dozens of children, I never once heard any of them cry.

On our off-times, we played games on the boat, fished for piranha, and even took a banana boat deep into the jungle with locals in the middle of the night to hunt for alligators. The lodging was tight and hot, and the food left plenty to be desired. Amazon catfish was one dish I hoped I'd never eat again in my life, but in light of the people we were serving, I had to be grateful to have food at all.

As soon as I returned home, I began preparing for the next mission trip. I made another mission trip with a group to Guatemala, and then one to Honduras. After those experiences, I decided to begin leading my own mission trips. I contacted people on the ground in different countries and made arrangements. I'd then take to social media and promote the trip and put out a general invitation. My goal was to include anyone who wanted to participate. Christians, atheists, Muslims, and Jews alike travelled together on my trips. My premise wasn't to beat a belief system into the locals, rather it was to promote God and love through action. In my mind it was a significantly more worthwhile to physically help people than to force our belief system onto a culture. By doing so, we often completed these trips feeling as if we were more fulfilled and reaped a greater benefit than the people we went to serve. We perhaps built a structure or brought them food and water, and we intentionally showed them love from strangers. But the impression they left on our hearts and the lessons of gratitude and humility we learned from them would last us a lifetime.

My trips usually consisted of anywhere from 10 to 20 people and would fill up rather quickly. I would simply go onto social media and announce an upcoming trip along with the details. Immediately, friends and strangers alike would contact me to sign up. The funny thing was people trusted me. I had established myself, this many years after being an addict and a criminal, to a place where people trusted their safety and/or the safety of their children to me in third world countries. I took this task very seriously. I would lay down my own life to preserve the lives I had been entrusted with.

Several years into leading these trips, I discovered Haiti, and my life was forever changed. We saw things in Haiti similar to a full out war zone. The area called Cite Soleil in Port Au Prince where we served was the poorest and largest slum in the Western Hemisphere. The slums stretched on for miles and consisted of zones reminiscent of those in *The Hunger Games* book and movie series. Certain zones were controlled by different gangs, and if one person wandered into a different zone, they were likely to get murdered. Trash stretched on for miles every in every direction. The rivers flowed with so much trash, you couldn't see the water underneath. People lived in tiny shacks haphazardly made from thrown together sheet metal, and others shacks were made from crumbling concrete. They consisted of one room with no furniture and a dirt floor. There was no electricity, no toilets, and no plumbing. The children ran around naked and malnourished with distended bellies, and they squatted on mountains of trash to relieve themselves while pigs rummaged nearby. There were decaying bodies in the rubble because there was nowhere to put them when they died, or were murdered. It was stiflingly hot every day, and we brought the one thing that could relieve it: fresh water.

Our funds helped pay for tanker trucks full of fresh water. So we would pull into the massive ghetto and hook up a hose to bring it to them. The children would come running to greet us as soon as they saw the truck pull up. They ran to us screaming "Hey you!" It was the only English words they knew. They climbed all over us and hugged us and tugged at us. They were mesmerized by our foreignness. They relished in the small things and found extreme joy in our smiles. They jumped to help us in any way they could, and they chased us up the street waving goodbye when we left. We brought them no toys or candy, only the water which their mothers gathered to retrieve from us. Often the only toys I saw the children play with were condoms.

The condoms had no doubt been distributed by some other missionaries to protect the women from having more children they couldn't afford. I knew this was an issue because several times adults placed babies in my arms and walked away, urging me to take them. There was nothing I could do. These people had been faced with the unimaginable decision to attempt to give their baby to a stranger so it could live, or keep it and watch it die. It was heart wrenching. The condoms that were intended to help stave off this situation were instead passed on to the children, who chewed on them and blew them into balloons frequently during the course of our work. I learned later that almost half of these children were slaves who had been sold off to other families in order to help their original parent continue to take care of their other siblings.

We came for a few hours then left. It broke our hearts every day when we had to leave them behind. I often wondered why they were so happy to see us come and so sad to see us go, and then I had a realization. Things weren't just bad there; they were extremely dark and miserable. The normal course of events in those neighborhoods more than likely consisted of violence, child abuse, and rape among other things. When the foreigners arrived with their big water trucks, we brought a sense of peace to the community. Everything that usually took place came to a standstill for just a couple of hours. And this, I presumed, was the reason the children loved us so much. It was all that we could do to love them back as much as we possibly could.

Meanwhile the women of the neighborhoods would line up along with the older children carrying everything from buckets, to plastic trashcans, to baby pools to fill with their weeks' ration of fresh water. It was what they had for the week to cook with, rinse with, and bathe with for their entire family.

Two of us would generally fill the buckets while the rest of us would help carry them back into the slums to their makeshift homes. The men would line the sides of the streets, sitting with each other and watching. I learned that in many of these extremely poor cultures it was customary for the men to do nothing, and usually drink all day, while the women and children did the majority of the labor. In an environment of sheer survival, it is often the stronger more dominant males who force the physically weaker women and children to labor for fear of violent repercussions. They sometimes looked at us and laughed, making comments amongst themselves and looking down on us because we were working alongside the women instead of relaxing like them. I embraced what they considered humiliation proudly.

We traveled all over Port Au Prince during our journeys to Haiti. We saw many things including dead babies, sick babies, children who were 10 and 12 years old, but looked like newborns because they had never received enough nourishment to grow. We saw babies who were left for dead in trash piles and children who were cast aside because of defects or because the voodoo religion believed they were cursed. We tended to them and loved on them all. We tended to the sick and dying elderly as well. When we returned from home from our trips to Haiti, we were forever changed. There is no explaining the draining emptiness that hovered over us for weeks following one of those trips. Almost every one of us felt a love for that country like we felt for no other.

Back home, I had not been around the bail bonds office as often, and things were starting to fall apart. I was losing my passion for making money and had fallen into my new passion of giving it away. Politics had stepped in and thrown a curveball at the bails bonds industry by attempting to eliminate cash bail, so judges and commissioners weren't setting them as often. My employees were losing interest and since I was away often, they took their jobs less seriously. Soon I started catching them in lies, petty thefts, and one of them even faked a full-blown robbery. I cleaned house and fired almost all of them in January 2015. The more that bail bonds began to claim the national spotlight as a new focus of political change, the more the bails decreased. I wasn't making money anymore. I had a little over a hundred thousand saved up, and I was running through it rather quickly through my travel and charity work.

I took on more projects and kept myself busy, always doing something to help the community. We drove truckloads of donations from Baltimore to Houston, TX when it flooded from hurricanes and again to the Carolinas when they had the same fate. I helped raise money for victims of house fires in our community, as well as other personal disasters. The holidays were busy with Thanksgiving feedings, and toy drives, and Christmas parties at low-income senior housing. Chasing my purpose had become a full-time, year-round job. Was this my purpose though, or was it a pursuit born from survivor's guilt? I survived something in those streets that not many come back from. I watched my peers die all around me. I survived overdoses and heart attacks when so many others didn't, and I avoided major prison sentences. Was I just trying to unravel a huge load of survivor's guilt that had bound me tight for years? Was I trying to right all the wrongs I'd done early in life? Was this just my attempt at undoing all of the bad karma I had created so many years ago? I liked to think that because I actually enjoyed doing this charity work that it was something much more pure. I preferred to call it gratitude.

After several years of leading all this mission and charity work, I decided to put a name to it. The Agape Projects became an official non-profit organization in order to add more legitimacy to these ventures. *Agape* is a Greek word for 'love in action' or 'God's love', and I added "projects" because of the versatility of the things that we did. There was never a direct area of service that we specialized in. This non-profit was meant to be a 'get in where we fit in' type of movement. The non-profit status literally didn't change a thing. We continued the same amount of marketing, and generally raised about the same amount of donations, and stuck with the model of 100% going back into the community. There were no salaried employees or money paid out for marketing. It was just a small homegrown passion birthed out of me chasing my purpose and gratitude for being alive and healthy when I didn't feel as though I'd earned that right.

As the bail bonds industry nearly came to a screeching halt through the coming year, I was left with more and more time on my hands. Money was running dry, but I couldn't stop the momentum I'd built. I was making an impact. Little old me, who sat in my school classes, invisible, too shy to speak. Sad old me, who had to use drugs and alcohol to become someone else because I didn't believe in the person I truly was. Wretched old me, who was homeless, addicted, and unwelcome in anyone's home. Tired old me, who couldn't seem to end his life, even when he wanted nothing more than death because the thought of living another week was unbearable. That same person was now putting joy into people's smiles and renewing faith in their hearts. How does one simply just lay that down?

It had been 30 years since those days of my youth where I had written poetry and short stories. It had been 25 years since I'd won the high school poetry contest and was simultaneously been expelled for selling drugs. It had been a long time since I'd sat down to write anything, and yet the calling was still within me. Since my youth I had always had a way with the English language and painted vivid pictures with my words. It was the one true gift that I had always felt certain God had given me, and I never really understood what to do with it. I always thought poetry was a thing of the Middle Ages, and there was no money in being a poet in modern society. I could write songs, but my singing voice sounded more like a drunken hyena than a nightingale. So I tossed my gift aside as a teenager and pursued illegal activities instead.

Now that I had a couple of decades of recovery under my belt and a message to share that could definitely help the people who were crawling down the lonely, painful road I once traveled, I knew I had to start writing again. The problem was I always had a strong fear of commitment. I would write a few pages, but never sit down to commit to something like a novel. I'd write a few pages, then quickly get sidetracked and never finish what I started. The itch to write was in me though, and I committed my mind to the mission ahead. One evening I went to a local Starbucks and sat in the corner and wrote a several-page story about my experience at a temazcal in Tulum. It was a sweat lodge in which I had a spiritual awakening in my new life of recovery. Then I wrote a twelve-page story about a wild day in my life of heroin use. That was it. I was fully committed. I had written over twenty pages. If I turned back now it was all for nothing. I knew exactly what I had to do.

I needed time and solitude. Not only that, but I would

need a safe space, away from all the trappings of the world around me, and most importantly from temptation. I was going to tell my whole story from the very beginning, detail by vivid detail. Doing so meant that I would be reliving all of the darkest, most miserable experiences of my life. If I wanted to do this the right way, it also meant I would be feeling all of those feelings all over again too: craving the drug, then feeling the withdrawal, the guilt, the shame and the suffering. I couldn't live my daily life while tapping back into my darkest moments and feeling them enough to be able to accurately describe them on paper. There was one obvious answer. I booked a two-week trip to Costa Rica.

My mother was living part time in Costa Rica now in the small town of Samara on the Nicoya Peninsula. It was about an hour south of Tamarindo. My parents had been looking for somewhere to retire outside of the US due to rising health-care costs. So, I brought them to Tamarindo to proudly show them my second home, and they fell in love with the country. Tamarindo, while pleasant during the day, had too much of a nightlife for them, so they began exploring the country on their own. They found the smaller beach town of Samara and decided that was where they wanted to start looking for a home. Samara was a much more natural setting, less developed, and quieter, but still had beaches, restaurants, and all of the local amenities one needed for a comfortable lifestyle. After going back and forth a couple times to look at houses and speak with local agents, they narrowed it down to a couple of houses they were interested in. I flew down with my father for a few days to look at the town and the houses myself. We stayed in a small house with an in-ground pool that sat at the top of a small mountain overlooking a lush valley. This house was secluded and yet only minutes from the town center and a host of different beaches. This was the home they decided to purchase.

For a couple of years they traveled back and forth and even tried their hand at making the home a part-time vacation rental. This was their future retirement home though, and they couldn't deal with the damage and disrespect imposed by vacationing tenants, and so that quickly ceased. After a few years my mother began spending several months a year living there, while my father came down for brief visits when he could slip away from work. He still had a few years before he could fully retire and they could call this their permanent paradise.

Costa Rica has a rainy season and a dry season. In the rainy season it rains every day, then from mid-November until the beginning of May it rarely rains a single drop. Just like at home, in the dry season there were way too many distractions for me in Costa Rica. I knew that if I were to get any writing accomplished, I had to fly in and stay there during the rainy season. In the month of October, the rains are the heaviest. There is a torrential downpour almost every day from morning to night, and this I decided, was the ideal time to get my writing done. My mother would also be there during the two weeks I planned to go, and I would need support just in case… The idea of being alone in that dark place while I wrote was enough to potentially swallow me whole. What I knew from years in recovery and a lifetime of battling anxiety and depression was that I had to always be aware of potential triggers and to be as prepared as possible to confront them. I would need to establish precautions and escape routes, if the need arose. Being in the middle of nowhere in the company of my mother, I was as protected as I possibly could be.

I flew into Costa Rica in the rain, and made the two-hour drive to their small house in Samara in the rain. I greeted my mother, got settled in, went to dinner, and the next morning with coffee in hand, I walked out to the small covered casita that overlooked the valley and began typing.

I woke up at dawn every morning and headed out to the casita to dive deeply into the remnants of my memory as I hammered away at the keyboard. Hummingbirds buzzed all around me, and howler monkeys climbed the trees in front of me eating leaves and screaming raucously. In spite of all the beauty around me, the beauty that I had run towards for comfort and solace, still a black cloud had enveloped me. It was as if the rain that poured unceasingly was a reflection of the memories that haunted my soul as I begun to dive deeper and deeper into a pained past. I'd type for maybe five or six hours a day. I started with my childhood and my own misdeeds, birthed from an apparent need to run from myself, and moved into my cycle of active addiction. The deeper I dove into my memory, the more vivid the memories became. Suddenly I was recalling the harshest times in my life, but not only was I remembering them, I was also feeling them all over again. The feelings of fear, hopelessness, and panic, the depression, guilt, and anxiety—it all swept over me. I was in a tropical paradise, but my mind had descended into a time warp back to Baltimore City in the late 1990s, including its streets, prisons, and rehabs. I felt every single feeling all over again, and because I sought complete authenticity, this is the way I wanted it.

When the rain stopped briefly at times, I would rush down to the beach and soak up the sun's rays before it tucked itself back behind the clouds again, or I would bathe the feelings away in the salty ocean froth. I'd walk the beach letting the sun bake off the remnants of my tortured past, and when the rain began to pour, I'd head back to the casita or to a local coffee bar and begin the descent all over again. As much as the town of Samara, Costa Rica was familiar to me, it was still a little foreign. I was a stranger in this world, and my soul wandered restlessly through the thick jungle air tangled in a dark web of anxiety and depression. Still, for once I had purpose, and I had to see this new mission all the way through. That alone was enough of a lamp to light the way for my soul's journey. At last, there was an end. And with the end came the exciting notion of sharing my story with the world.

After two weeks and a couple hundred pages typed, the time had come for me to fly home. I was empty, yet full. I had accomplished so much, and yet I was only halfway there. I had been living with a girlfriend at the time who had moved into my house with me. When I shared with her my need to finish this project, she said, "Go Dan, don't let me hold you back." It was exactly what I needed to hear from her. After a week at home, I flew back to Costa Rica for the remainder of October to finish my book. I had successfully bared my soul on paper for all to see. Transparency, honesty, and telling it all—the good, the bad, and the shameful—was my objective, and I had done it in 465 pages.

The art of storytelling is a labor of love. I had no idea at the time whether or not telling a story would be lucrative. I imagined that if I sold enough copies that I stood to turn a profit. What I did not consider were the extensive costs that go into creating a book the right way. I would need to pay for editing, proofreading, design, marketing, and a ton of other services. I was told that self-publishing could get my book out almost instantly, whereas going through a traditional publisher would take years. Traditional publishing could stand to be more profitable in the long run, however the heroin epidemic was wiping away lives in our community daily. So I decided if this book could reach even one life, then it had to be released immediately. I paid in pieces with the money that trickled in from my failing business, and as the beginning of 2019 approached, I had paid over $10,000 in costs to get my book ready for release and was eagerly awaiting the last stages. I then created my own publishing company called "Phoenix Rising Publishing" for the financial management of the proceeds and expenses of the book. Phoenix Rising is symbolic of my journey and resurrection from my own ashes and a rebirth, just as the phoenix did in legend.

In June of 2019 I finally had a printed copy of *Chasing A Flawed Sun* in hand, and shortly thereafter it was released for sale on Amazon. I hosted a couple of book signings, and as people read my story, it continued to spread by word of mouth. I was featured on several news stations. The book was named Baltimore's Best Book of the Year in 2020. I also made an appearance on Good Morning Washington and had an episode of the 700 Club dedicated to me, and yet none of those instances reflected a spike in sales. Word of mouth carried the book to the far reaches of the planet, and within two years approximately 50,000 copies have sold. It opened up doors for me to speak at jails, hospitals, funerals, suicide conferences, addiction events, churches and more. I had gotten a PO Box specifically designated for the business of the book and was surprised to receive letters from readers as far as Scotland and Venezuela, as well as from inmates all over the United States of America. I was no world renowned author, I wasn't even a blip on the radar of known authors. But coming from where I had, a little boy who hated himself and was too shy to step out of the shadows, to an adult who was a plague upon society and mostly himself, to a destitute addict who wished for nothing but escape and to trade places with those who were dying around him, to become a beacon of light was amazing. I was lighting a path for all those who were wandering the dark wilderness that I had crawled out of. I was finally chasing my one true sun. Not only chasing it, but I had learned how to harness it and share it with the world. This was yet another step up the ladder of purpose. This, I was convinced, was one of the reasons that I survived what I shouldn't have survived.

TRANSPARENCY & HONESTY
IN THE AFTERMATH

THE ANXIETY AND depression I struggled with my whole life has never disappeared. There is no known formula to make it vanish entirely. I've tried every natural remedy, including exercise, yoga, chasing my life purpose, and everything in between. While all of these activities help to hold it at bay, I've never truly ridded myself of it. For twenty years I have taken Paxil (paroxetine) for these issues, and yet they still come at me hard from time to time. I have gone days forgetting to take my medication on a vacation before, and the anxiety and depression come flooding in at an unbearable rate, leaving me panic stricken and incapable of functioning. This, I know, is my blessing and my curse.

I have learned to live by the serenity prayer of accepting the things that I cannot change and changing the things that I can. After time and time again trying to manage my anxiety with outside means, I have finally come to the notion that the only thing I can change is my reaction to it and my perspective regarding it. It comes at times when life is smooth, and it rattles me to the core. It makes me wish for death. It makes me cry out for mercy. It makes me cry and tremble in fear. Most of all it is impalpable, coming in without warning or cause. What it does do, though, is keep me humble. For that I appreciate it. I change my perception to be thankful for it. It is through our worst pain that we grow stronger, and this I must remember when I am shaken to the core.

I have tried other means to manage anxiety and depression and the disruptions they bring. I have looked for escape routes, but they always lead me to even darker places. Out of desperation I have tried all different kinds of chemical cures, even when I should have known better, but nothing seems to make it go away. Self-medicating through my late teens and early twenties with alcohol and heroin only made it worse day by day. In my late thirties, years into recovery, doctors recommended I try marijuana for my anxiety and depression. Marijuana had never been a drug of choice for me. As a teenager when all of my friends smoked weed, and I chose alcohol. I hated the high marijuana gave me; it made me tired or it brought on anxiety attacks. But now in this modern era, a shift has been made. Medical marijuana dispensaries have opened up all over Maryland, and I have friends who opened some. The professionals I was doing business with were suddenly open about their marijuana use. Lawyers, doctors, nurses, and other professionals would tell me things like, "You just need to find the right strain of marijuana. It will make your anxiety go away."

I opened a juice bar in 2019 in East Baltimore where we sold smoothies, açaí bowls, and fresh juices. I had heard about CBD, a non-psychotropic part of the marijuana plant, being used for anxiety. I ordered some and created our own CBD smoothie for sale at the juice bar. We mixed several green vegetables and some fruits along with hemp seeds and CBD, and it sold very well. People were raving about the effects of the CBD and its harmlessness. I began to take some, and after a few months experimenting with a variety of recommended doses, I felt absolutely no difference. Apparently, it works well for some and not others.

Still another doctor recommended I try marijuana. I started to rationalize that it was medicine and that I was not using the marijuana as an escape. Rather it would be used strictly to quell my anxiety, it was doctor recommended and by no means an addictive drug that I had a history with. I bought a vape pen with a suggested strain of marijuana and hit it one night. At first I was struck by intense anxiety as the high took over my body, but once I crossed the threshold and the high settled in, I felt at extreme peace. I was cradled by the high and felt comfortable. I drifted easily off to sleep at night without a care in the world. It was a great experience, and I told myself I would only resort to it in times of extreme need, maybe once or twice a month.

Within two weeks I was doing it daily. It began to consume my every thought. I woke up in the morning thinking about it and anticipating when I could hit the vape pen. I began doing it not only every day, but earlier and earlier each day. Soon it caused worse anxiety. I tried different strains to no avail. Everyone had an opinion on why it wasn't working and which strain I needed. Sometimes it would give me such bad anxiety that I would leave it alone for months, then after a bunch of unsolicited advice from friends or people in the field, I'd go back for another round. It never worked. It was the same cycle of addiction and irrational behavior I had experienced before with addictive substances. I had to cut myself off for good. But I wasn't ready to let it go entirely.

I made a pact with myself that I would only smoke weed when I was out of the country on vacations. This meant I would only be smoking a few times a year to open and expand my mind while I was in paradise. Instead, as my next trip to Costa Rica approached, I was no longer looking forward to my time in paradise. Rather, all I could think about was the opportunity to smoke weed when I got there. Normally the night before I leave on vacation I am filled with anticipation, like a child on Christmas Eve, with visions of white sand beaches and freedom. This time, however, I awaited with trepidation, and the only thing on my mind was going to the Rastas that sold weed on the beach as soon as possible. It became an obsession no different than the one I had to get alcohol or heroin years before, an obsession to leave reality for a place I imagined to be so much safer.

When the plane landed and I was escorted to the rental car kiosk, I found myself asking the people there where to buy marijuana. I was acting like a fiend. I drove the two hours to Samara, but instead of going to the house to unload my luggage, I went straight to the beach, bought some weed and a bowl and lighter and smoked in the car. The next morning, I went to the beach alone and sat on the sand smoking the bowl, then walked out into the waves. I was the only one on Carrillo Beach. The water around me sparkled like a billion little diamonds, the sun shone down on me, and I began talking to God. It was one of the most spiritual moments of my life. I had never felt so good, standing in that water, just me and God, alone and uplifted. I felt like I had reached enlightenment and a thousand angels were there with me. I finally left the water and laid down on my towel in sheer ecstasy. I continued to smoke.

The next day I had a nervous breakdown in paradise. It was the weed. The day before was its last gift to me. I awoke with the revelation that marijuana would never be for me. It was driving me crazy, stealing my identity, and ruining my life. It left me with anxiety, desperation, and suicidal thoughts.

I poured those feelings out to my mother and confessed my new obsession. I gave my bowl and marijuana to a girl in town and vowed to never smoke it again. I instantly felt mountains of relief, and the depression and anxiety faded. My God has created me for the struggle, this I know. There is no easy way out. There are no shortcuts.

Alcohol, heroin, methadone, marijuana, pills, kratom, and anything else that creates a shortcut to avoid inner and outer struggle is, in a sense, a poison. Not only did they stunt my emotional growth, but they eventually destroyed me and everything I had built. We are designed to grow through struggle, like a seed pushing against the dirt to bloom, like muscles formed in the gym—everything on this planet grows stronger through struggle and pressure. All of these drugs were tools to help me avoid the struggle, consequently stunting my growth and doing a disservice to my very existence. If there is one thing I am sure of, with my whole soul, it is that we are put on this Earth to grow stronger through our experiences here, then we discard these bodies and return to our God greater and stronger than we were when we came. For me, using these shortcuts to avoid my struggles defeated the very purpose of my existence. I was running from the things I was destined to face. God wasn't going to let me do that, not without severe repercussions. Anxiety and depression were the worst repercussions I ever faced, worse than any pain or loss.

HOW DO YOU FIND...

THE QUESTION ARISES: How does one find joy in the normalcy of everyday life, in the simplicities of ups and downs, after experiencing nirvana? After the absolute pinnacle of elation from the dopamine dump that follows the hissing and crackling of a smoldering crack rock melting, and its cool smoke enveloping your lungs? Or the icy shot of cocaine that sprints through your capillaries, clutching your racing heart, and carrying your floating mind out past heaven's narrow gates? After the bitter drip or warm breath of a heroin rush as it takes control of your body, and settles you into a mindless Eden in which the gravity of this world suspends the cells within you in much the same way that it holds you without? How do you find comfort in a reckless world after being cocooned in the inner blanket of security that no outer comforter comes close to mimicking? Even the freedom of a careless alcohol-induced night of dancing and adventure does not compare to the best night sober and the inevitable wrestling with anxiety and insecurity. How, after you've touched the pinnacle of freedom and comfort and elation, do you even hope to find meaning in the ups and downs of a normal life, particularly when access to those unparalleled experiences is always close within reach?

It's simple. The key to the ultimate freedom is found in purpose. And when it comes to purpose, slow and steady wins the race. When I stumbled into a life of recovery, I had no purpose. I had simply given up. I had tried over and over and over again to use successfully, to drink, to sell drugs, to do anything except take the long hard road of living life in any semblance of normalcy. I fell so far behind by trying to take shortcuts through life that it seemed impossible to catch up to where I should have been as a 25-year-old man. That, of course, is judging by society's standards. There are no standards by which we should judge ourselves or anyone else at 16, 18, or 25. There is an idea and a pressure that society imposes on us to adhere to a certain timeline and level of accomplishment, parameters by which society defines success. It took me many years to understand that society's definition of success means nothing.

Each of us encounter our own internal struggles, accomplishments, and timelines. Our success is determined by how we manage, overcome and survive our struggles. In the beginning, I couldn't see that. Therefore, I had extremely low confidence and self-esteem. Of course, being the ego driven creatures that we are, I never allowed myself to believe or understand that I had low self-esteem. In fact, I did quite the opposite and overcompensated with cockiness and arrogance to cover up the failure I felt deep within.

The pride and egotistical notion I created of myself kept me alive for a very long time. It protected me. It pushed me to appear outwardly strong, to refuse to give anyone the satisfaction of seeing me fail and fall. If I was serving my ego, I certainly couldn't feed an addiction at the same time. Even though both were harmful to me, I couldn't serve both of them at the same time because one built me up outwardly, while the other destroyed me outwardly. In this way, I used fire to fight fire. I did this for many years until my fragile walls finally collapsed, and I had a brief alcohol relapse many years later.

I started out as an innocent child, building walls of ego around myself during my teenage years to hide my fears and insecurities. I quickly became egocentric. I hurt people and used people to make myself feel better. Then heroin broke me. When I emerged from my war with heroin, I was faced with real life all over again. Fear and insecurity were back in control. I returned to my layers of ego to protect myself and hide my weakness for many years until I had the epiphany that there was more to this life. I had survived a substance-filled existence for a reason. I had a purpose. From that realization forward, recovery began as a peeling back of the layers, taking down each one of the walls I had forged to protect myself from myself. True recovery is a journey into oneself, to understand and find the original you. It is a return to innocence.

My journey back to the original me has been the most exciting one of all. There is nothing more uplifting than accomplishment and success when it is rightfully and honestly earned. Once we learn we are able to succeed and that we can push through obstacles, encouragement comes. When we explore the jungles of self-doubt, when we machete-hack our way through the impossible undergrowth of our fear and step through virgin territories, the journey becomes inwardly exhilarating. I've stepped out onto the peak of accomplishment and looked at the expanse of rugged terrain that got me here, and I have been empowered with elation. It's hard to believe that little old me made it here, and I did so, just trekking and hacking, and sweating, and almost breaking, one day at a time.

At the beginning of this chapter, I asked how anything could possibly compare to the dopamine dump, invincibility, or painlessness of being drunk or high. Chasing down and fulfilling purpose does. We all have purpose, especially those of us who have made it through the fiery struggles of addiction, disease, war, or any affliction in which the odds are stacked against us. For some, finding purpose may be a crystal-clear vision. For others like me, it may be completely nebulous, a journey in and of itself trying to figure out exactly what it is. The journey becomes addictive. Accomplishment becomes addictive. Overcoming obstacles becomes addictive. And suddenly we aren't running from fear any longer, instead we are facing it head on, excited to see what possibilities lie around every corner. And then we slowly begin to love ourselves. This is the recovery that I know.

THE OPPOSITE EFFECT

WHEN I WAS young and in active addiction somebody said to me, "You know if you don't like the way your life is going, then you need to start doing the opposite of everything you are doing now." It seemed like a simple, obvious observation, one that I brushed off at the time, and yet it always stuck with me.

Years later, I began to take it to heart. It's quite a simple formula, but life and success are always quite simple at the core. It's us humans who complicate things by overthinking, and our overthinking comes from fear. A life full of love is the most rewarding life, and love, while complex, is quite simple at its core. A life of addiction is a life filled with fear, while a life filled with success and happiness is a life of love. The opposite of love is not hate; it is fear. There may be a thin line between love and hate, but there's a chasm between love and fear. As I said in my last book, recovery is a tight rope walk, in which we carefully cross the chasm between the two, slowly moving into a realm of love while putting more distance between ourself and our old life of fear.

The first, and most obvious behavior we must reverse is drugs or alcohol use. If we used drugs and alcohol before, and they brought negative impacts upon our life, then very simply the first step in the opposite effect, to stop using them. Easier said than done, right? It is the largest initial chasm to a life of recovery, and fear fights us hard to keep most of us from crossing. Most addicts are not ready or willing to put down the drugs/alcohol until beaten into submission. The fear of never using or drinking again, and having to face withdrawals, consequences, and learning to live life sober keeps us from even attempting to stop, no matter how badly we may want to. Even if we do stop briefly, we run back to the drugs or alcohol with the intent of trying to control our usage after the first time we face fear again.

So, the first step is to stop. No matter how you get to this point, stop. Realize, drugs and alcohol are not the problem. They are just the means by which we medicate the problem. Drugs and alcohol don't hurt anyone sitting on the shelf by themselves. They don't hurt the addict or non-addict. Drug and alcohol usage is only an indicator of a greater underlying issue. Unless we learn how to identify the symptoms that lead us to self-destruction in the first place, we will never fully find freedom and happiness. There is a difference between addicts and the social users. There is a reason some people take pain medication and don't continue to use it until it destroys their lives, or some people can have an occasional drink, and others cannot. It is generally found in the 'why.' Why do we use? We may have started out drinking socially but found that it was an easy way to hide self-doubt, to run from fear, to bury feelings, or to become someone we thought we liked better than our sober selves. Maybe we relied on drugs to overcome social anxiety, to bury depression, to be more confident, or to escape reality as often as possible. Whatever the 'why' we cover, hide, or pause it with substance abuse. Then when we stop using drugs and alcohol, all of our 'whys' come flooding back with even more intensity than before. Only now, they have been stifled for so long that we run back to using in order to repress them further. And the cycle continues. We've never learned how to correctly address our fears. Finally, it gets to the point where drugs and alcohol have robbed us of our true lives. They have destroyed us, and we have no choice but to quit or die.

Once we have completed the first task by stopping our drug/alcohol abuse, we are confronted again with raw, sober reality and all the feelings that come with it. Instead of running back to our drug of choice to escape our fears, we have to respond differently. We have to do the opposite of using drugs. In the rooms of the anonymous programs, you'll be advised to: "Go to a meeting," or "Call your sponsor," or "Pick up the phone and call anyone," if you feel like using. There is no stronger power than having other human beings in recovery to hold us accountable. Sure we can pray, meditate, go to the gym, go for a walk, but we cannot trust ourselves and our motives this early on. We've spent years in active addiction unable to trust ourselves. Our best decisions brought us self-destruction and misery. We've lied to ourselves countless times. We can't expect those behaviors to suddenly change. Being by ourselves in early recovery, especially when the desire to escape hits us, is a dangerous game to play. Once we've gained some time in sobriety and built some self-trust, we can begin to map out other ways to address a desire for escape, like the ones I mentioned above.

Before we can trust ourselves and our own decisions, we must build self-confidence and prove our value to ourselves. This took many, many years for me. Although, I thought I was extremely confident in early recovery, I was still lying to myself. My cockiness and inflated image were just a fragile wall that I erected to protect that scared little child inside who lacked a feeling of self-worth. In reality there was no way I walked out of a life of misery and destitution with no real plan for the future and thought I was as important and as strong as I did. I was still deceiving myself.

We must build momentum. We start out in recovery and move through life almost spinning, not knowing which direction to pursue. The world of possibilities out here is huge, and many of us feel like lost children. We are stranded so far behind our peers because the world continued moving while we remained stagnant. I dropped out of high school, never learned a trade or a skill, did virtually nothing with my whole life by society's standards. Most of my peers were married, had careers, children, and houses as I was coming out of addiction. I had lost a decade of my life and maturation. It's easy to give up when faced with our despair once we see how far we've fallen behind. It's also easy to get impatient and try to rush ahead to make up for lost time, only to find ourselves floundering, frustrated, and sulking with a victim mentality when we don't get there fast enough.

The world owes us nothing. We don't deserve accolades or special treatment for taking the hard road that everyone else took once we come to the conclusion that the wrong route left us failing miserably. We come into recovery like a person who spilled a drink and made a big mess, and then expect people to clap for us and congratulate us for cleaning it up. When we don't get the applause we think we deserve, we pout about it and whine that life isn't fair. This is victim mentality, and it will keep a person stuck in a cycle of self-annihilation.

The good news is that there is no timeline. We all have our own pace on our own journeys. Each of us was put here to live out our own story. Every one of us will face different struggles in life, and our timeline is unique to us. Too often society projects the idea that you need to be married by a certain age, have a career by a certain age, and babies by a certain age and on and on. This is a manmade, and often cultural, concept behind. It is not a golden standard by which to judge yourself or anyone else. How can we possibly compare our timeline to someone else's, someone who perhaps didn't face the same struggles we faced, or make the same choices we made? God's timeline for you was written before you were even born, and it will unfold just as planned. Your soul was put here to face its own unique battles and grow from them and then return home when it's evolved. You cannot put a manmade timeline on that. Be patient.

This momentum I mentioned above, like any momentum, involves first moving a heavy object, and that object is ourselves. Like anything else we want to move, we must first decide which direction we are going with it. Very simply, there are two directions: life or death. Every moment of every day I get to choose: Will this decision help me to live a better life or die a little? Every single decision, every day can be narrowed down to that one question. Will this help build me or destroy me? If we've managed to make a quality decision to stop drinking or using drugs, then the path is clear, we want to live. Every decision from that point forward should continue to push us in that direction. Like most heavy objects, it will be hard to move at first, perhaps even seem immobile. But if we are persistent, we will begin to feel slight movement in the right direction, and we'll slowly pick up pace. The faster we move in the direction of life, the harder it is to stop the movement and begin to move backwards. Imagine a train barreling down the tracks in one direction. How hard would be to first stop the train, then move it in the opposite direction? This is the momentum with which we want to create our lives. We are moving so forcibly in the direction of success, happiness, and life that it will be extremely hard for anything to reverse our direction. Eventually, in keeping with the law of motion, we will increase our momentum in the direction of life, so it becomes easier to move in that direction; it takes less and less effort. It becomes natural to us. With enough momentum, there is no mountain we can't climb. No struggle in this life will be able to turn us around. We may need to put effort back in at times, but we can be unstoppable.

The opposite effect is how I built and continue to build my momentum. I have learned to apply the opposite effect in virtually every area of my life from social, mental, spiritual, physical, to financial. I aim to live and grow within every one of these areas daily, rather than die in them. When we want to move a large object, we must apply pressure to all crucial areas to keep the whole object moving in one direction. Leave no stone unturned. Remember the saying I picked up in early addiction: "If you don't like the course in which your life is heading, then do the opposite of everything you are doing now." That means everything. Addiction may seem like it's just drugs and alcohol on the surface, but remember substance abuse is just a symptom of a greater underlying illness that creeps in and affects every single aspect of your life.

THE SOCIAL OPPOSITE

My behavior under the influence of alcohol hurt everyone around me. I was nasty and violent, and I lashed out. I physically hurt and stole from people. I got high on drugs and became a manipulative, and anti-social liar. Now every day of my life, I practice honesty in every form. I'm brutally honest. I give instead of take. I practice selflessness until it becomes habit. I'm kind to people as often as possible. In 20 years of working recovery, I have rarely ever had the need to get physically violent with someone, and yet when I drank it was a nightly occurrence. It wasn't easy. I suffered and still suffer from insecurity and social anxiety. I wasn't cured of these things overnight. However, I had to break down barriers and take social chances. I had to open up to people if I wanted to do the opposite of what I had previously done. Being a warrior, living the intended life of recovery, and receiving the blessings from it is all about facing our fears head on. This is how we grow. This is how the human soul evolves. This is our core purpose. I had to take risks with my fear and sign myself up for social situations that would make me uncomfortable. I had to put myself out there and make friends with people I wouldn't normally be friends with. I had to start hanging out with the opposite kinds of people I hung out with in my old life. I had to do these things until they became habit and were no longer something I had to force.

Soon I started having friendships and relationships with people who were a lot deeper than those I tried to make connections with in the bars and the drug world. Soon I found people who accepted me and liked me for me, rather than what I could offer them in the moment. This would do wonders for my self-esteem. Doing the social opposite slowly built my self-image in a real way, which is an essential need in a successful life of recovery. I began to feel the opposite about myself than what I had felt in years prior.

My friends and I were social misfits. We relied on alcohol to be our social lubricant. I was a quiet, sketchy, nervous kid until alcohol helped me blossom into a wild, violent, womanizing party animal. Heroin took away my fear and my social anxiety. Once sober, I had to push myself to learn how to go through life without these crutches. I had to relearn how to function in society. Not only that, I needed to learn how to be the opposite of the monster drugs and alcohol had made me.

THE PHYSICAL OPPOSITE

As a using addict, I neglected everything except the quest to get more and more of my drug of choice, whether it was alcohol or heroin or cocaine. My health took a major backseat. I was often malnourished, or my diet was horrible. I never once set foot in a gym. Once I got clean, I began to do the opposite.

I joined a gym, focused on working out and getting into shape. I began rethinking the foods I was eating. It took me ten years, but I eventually quit smoking cigarettes. All of my decisions involved making healthy choices for myself and my appearance. I did the opposite of what I did in my old life. Instead of putting my health on the back burner and neglecting doctor visits, I began paying attention to what I ate, took care of my body, and saw healthcare professionals whenever needed. This not only improved my outward appearance, but it increased that very important piece to my recovery: my self-esteem.

THE MENTAL OPPOSITE

LIKE EVERY OTHER area of my body, my mental health suffered big time under the use of drugs and alcohol. I never stimulated my brain except to use it to devise schemes to attain money to get more drugs. I poisoned myself with copious amounts of alcohol and drugs until I was borderline brain dead on a nightly basis. So when I came into recovery, I had to start doing the opposite. I read books, I do crosswords and other puzzles daily, I dream up and create legal business ideas. I challenge myself mentally as often as possible in healthy ways. You might do so through your career or your social circle, even through social media. The point is that we weren't using our brains, rather we were killing them in active addiction and alcoholism. We now must reverse the damage and start building them up by using them as much as possible. The more books I read, the more puzzles I solve, the more arguments I win, the greater the impact and advancement I experience in my careers and undertakings by thinking my way through problems instead of running from them. Subsequently, the more my self-esteem, yet again, begins to flourish.

THE SPIRITUAL OPPOSITE

I HAD AN understanding of God when I was in the streets, but I had no relationship with Him. A relationship is a two-way street, a give and take. I made my relationship with God essentially about begging to get out of whatever trouble or sickness or dark hole of anxiety and depression I found myself in. Not once did I give praise or gratitude, or humility, or even change the behavior that led me to that place to begin with. I moved through life with reckless abandon not caring who I hurt, and then when reality caught up with me, I hit my knees with tears in my eyes and begged God, "Please don't let me go to jail," or "Please take away my dope sickness." Each prayer was a momentary plea for mercy with no action behind them. Some prayers were simple and sincere like, "Please God, I don't want to get high anymore. Please don't let me use again tomorrow." But I never took the action required to make such a request possible. I only prayed for a miracle. God moves mountains, but you must bring a shovel. Without willingness to face your fears and actually take action to change, you are simply going through the motions to make yourself feel better in the moment.

So when I got clean, I immediately began doing the opposite. I built a relationship with the God of my understanding. I began to look within, to take accountability for my own actions. I began a spiritual journey within myself to understand why I do the things I do, and how I can change poor behaviors. In my life of drinking and using, I never once stopped to analyze my motives, to learn about myself, or work on inner growth. I was choosing death. Once I decided to do the opposite, I committed to start understanding who I really was. This is the same spiritual journey of self that the twelve steps of the anonymous programs are designed to guide you through.

The old me would get mad and lash out violently at someone with harsh words. The new me would get mad and think, "How does this person hold enough power over me to get me so angry? What is the real reason I am even angry? How can I properly address it?" No one can truly make you angry but yourself; only you hold that power. It is the same for almost any emotion. This inner exploration falls under spiritual health and the notion of God, our Creator, because the more we learn about ourselves, the closer we get to finding out who we are and who we were meant to be, and the closer we come to our Creator and their intentions for us.

I believe one of the biggest obstacles affecting a person's ability to stay clean and live a successful, happy life in recovery is personal accountability. This also falls under the spiritual aspect of self-exploration. As addicts/alcoholics we are often consumed with a victim mentality. It is everyone else's fault that we are the way we are. We were dealt a bad hand at life. We suffered trauma when we were young. We have depression, anxiety, come from a broken home, lost our job, were cheated on, and on and on... The fact of the matter is that there are millions of people who have been through the same circumstances or worse who didn't become drug addicts or alcoholics. The major difference I notice between those who live successful lives in recovery and those who continue to actively use or repeatedly relapse is their level of personal accountability.

I finally dropped the victim mentality and began taking personal responsibility for every single decision I made in life and for every circumstance I found myself in. I no longer blame circumstances, or my parents, or my mental health, or anything else for my previous use. I take responsibility if an employer fires me, or a partner leaves me, or another driver cuts me off. If I get angry or react, I take responsibility for my reaction. By acknowledging that everything that happens to me is a result of my decisions, I've learned I am actually a creator. In a spiritual sense, God created humans in the likeness of His image, therefore we too are creators. We can create the life we want and control our response to the world around us. It is up to us whether our circumstances are favorable, or painful and negative.

Our perspective holds the key to our future. I simply shifted my perspective and chose gratitude instead of acting out like a victim and pointing the finger. Learning that I am responsible for everything that happens to me is empowering. It is a wakeup call and can do wonders for building up our self-esteem. Instead of losing a job and going into a spiral of depression, beating ourselves up, and eventually using, we can shift our perspective. Sure, maybe I lost that job. I could've done better. I could have been such a great employee that they wouldn't have added me to their lay-off roster. At least I got that experience. At least I'm not homeless and getting high. Maybe this will lead to opening the door to something bigger and better. Maybe I needed a break so I can focus on finding my purpose. This applies to anything in life. The same world looks a lot different to different people, and it's all because of perspective. Once we shift our perspective from victim to creator, a world of possibilities will open up before us.

THE FINANCIAL OPPOSITE

FINANCIALLY, MY LIFE was a mess in active addiction. I couldn't manage money. My goal everyday was finding just enough money to get drunk or high, sink into the abyss for the evening, only to start all over the next day from square one. It took me awhile to get the momentum going in this area after I got clean because I had no trade or experience doing anything legal. In the beginning I lived paycheck to paycheck, just to give myself the outward appearance of success. It was all a deception. Not only was I deceiving others, but I was deceiving myself. It wasn't until years into recovery that I began to focus on building multiple avenues of income, saving money and re-investing it, and giving money back into the community selflessly. My personal timeline was long here because my lack of skill meant lack of opportunity. But I got creative, and when I found a niche, I honed in on it and gave it everything I had. There are opportunities out there for all of us. We must be patient and creative. We can't reasonably expect to destroy our lives for years, ravage the communities around us, then suddenly gain wealth or even catch up to our peers in weeks. I see more people relapse and give up because they can't catch up with their peers within a short time after they achieve sobriety. Patience and humility will keep us clean and sober until the opportunity to achieve financial success eventually presents itself. We simply cannot afford to give up.

Once I finally achieved enough financial stability so I no longer lived check to check, worried about paying bills, or stressed over keeping a roof over my head, I began to give back. I started helping in a soup kitchen and then at a homeless shelter. After that I began donating not only my time, but my money. I began doing the opposite of what I did in my prior life. Instead of stealing from the community, I gave to it. Instead of harming the community, I did my best to heal it. Instead of being selfish, I began to be selfless. I was on a quest to undo all the wrongs I had done—if that was even possible. As my mission grew, I began donating large sums of money and championing causes for the poor and underprivileged. By doing so, I had became the opposite of what I once was. I became a role model instead of a scourge on society. I was someone who people looked up to rather than looked down upon. It became my new addiction, but this addiction was okay because it was the opposite of my old one. My old addiction was self-centered. My new one is completely about giving of myself. This, I know, can only help keep the momentum going.

I could go on and on about the ways in which I reversed the course of action in countless areas of my life. Instead of hiding from and or using my family, I have rebuilt solid relationships with them. Instead of cheating on women, I became a loyal partner. Instead of being an unproductive employee, I became an asset. I intentionally focused on being the opposite of who I once was in every single area of my life. As a result, my entire life has become the opposite of what it once was. I have started and owned a few businesses. I am president of my own nonprofit. I have traveled to 32 countries so far, led 16 mission trips, and have written a book that has sold almost a hundred thousand copies. I have succeeded at almost everything I have put my mind to in recovery. I have built amazing relationships and married a beautiful woman. I couldn't have ever imagined any of this. Yet I say none of this to brag. I share this to offer perspective. I was a bottom-of-the-barrel, homeless junkie who no one ever thought would live to see 20 years of age. I never thought I'd live past that age, much less find happiness, success, and purpose. It is possible for everyone. It simply begins with a shift in perspective, followed by a shift in behavior. And the momentum you create will take you wherever you let it.

Happiness lies within the journey. Very rarely do we set out on a journey and only find happiness once we reach our goal. It isn't in our nature. Once we achieve our goal, we almost immediately set our sights on something further, then set out in search of that. We are happiest when we are on the hunt, knee-deep in the moment, living and breathing our desire to achieve what we set out for. When man finally does reach the elusive treasure chest at the end of the rainbow, he is left disappointed and empty, and seeks something new to find. It's in our DNA to get caught up in the quest and always thirst for more.

Life is a never-ending journey for us, and the elusive white steed in the forest is our purpose. Each and every one of us has a divine purpose, especially those of us who have been through hell and back, who have survived an addiction that most do not. If you are still alive and here today, there is no question in my mind that you still have a purpose to fulfill. For some, it may be right in front of you. It may smack you right in the head one day as obvious as can be. Yet for others like myself, we may scramble trying to guess at what our purpose is, trying our best to find it and fulfill it. For me, it very well may be writing books, or it may be it's charity work, or being a role model. For others it may be changing the world in some other way, or it may be as simple as being a mother, a daughter, a son, or a teacher. Your purpose is God given, and it is the biggest reward your recovery could ever give you. I urge you to climb upon your horse, head out into the forests of life, and draw your bow, ready to chase your purpose until your God calls you home. It is in the chase that true happiness will be found and in the momentum of recovery, reaching an almost unstoppable speed.

But those who hope in the Lord
will renew their strength.
They will soar on wings like eagles; they
will run and not grow weary,
they will walk and not be faint.

—Isaiah 40:31

WAVES

I HAD A dream. In fact, I had many dreams. They surfed along my brain waves, rising, crashing, then pulling back across my grey matter. They swelled and then spilled out over me. Their sudden roar woke me, startled me, and I lay there staring up at the piercing sun. It bore down upon me as if looking straight through me and into my soul. A bead of sweat ran off my forehead and into my eye as I tilted my head to look to my side. I squinted. Endless sand stretched out to my left until it met the lapping seashore. I twisted my head to look the other direction and was met with the same sight. There was no sign of life in either direction, not even a gull in the sky above me. Just a repetitive crash and hiss as the water kissed the hot sand, then pulled back like sheets exposing an empty bed beneath.

My skin was hot and would soon be burnt. I must not have been laying there for too long, or I'd have been coated in blisters. The sun was intense out there and seemed to focus on my frail body. The beams reached out like lasers painting my skin with heat. I twisted and writhed until I came to all fours on the grainy, hot sand below me in order to give my face and chest a break from the glare and to better survey my surroundings. Craning my head to look up, I clearly saw tracks that indicated I had crawled to this place. My eyes traced their trajectory through the white sand and up over the small crest of a hill until it reached a patch of greenery beyond. As they raised even further, my stomach dropped and feelings of horror overtook me as I looked at the jungle beyond and remembered exactly where I had come from. Beyond the first line of trees, foliage, and vines, was nothing but a quiet, eerie darkness that seemed to beckon me back in.

My pulse raced, and I was flooded with sadness and despair. Then the waves washed those feelings away, and I was left empty inside, helpless on the beach. I couldn't go back to where I'd been. It wasn't even a fragment of a possibility for me. I turned away from the jungle. I couldn't even look at it.

I faced the opposite direction to look at the ocean before me. I knew what I had to do; it was my only means of escape. My entire life had led me to this. I had been beaten and dragged, and I had failed over and over again. My former mission was a waste of time. I had to end my senseless suffering. I placed one hand in front of the other and crawled slowly towards the ocean. I began to move as quickly as I could, scurrying on all fours through the sand. I couldn't even stop my thoughts long enough to feel the scorching sand on my knees and hands. I was too fixated on the ocean and the goal ahead of me. As my palms began to meet the cooler sand, then the water in front of me, I crawled even faster. Then I closed my eyes and tore into the salty water on all fours like a dog racing into a spraying hose. The difference being that the refreshment I was seeking wasn't meant to give me life; it was meant to take me under. I planned to crawl into this sweet ocean and into its undertow until I reached a point of no return. I prayed that the currents would carry me off into my final freedom. The jungle broke me. The sun burnt me. I was ready to surrender my life to the waves.

The water smashed into my face. I tasted its salt. Soon it

was over my head, yet I crawled even further. I crawled past the waves until the world fell silent around me. I crawled past my fears, and my pain, deep into a quiet place where there was nothing at all. I crawled across that sandy ocean floor until the panic from my lack of oxygen began to consume me. I couldn't save myself. I absolutely couldn't. There was no way I could willingly return. I had to surrender to the panic, to the fear, to the pain and just float. As I drifted, I drifted out of consciousness...

When I awoke, I was heaving and coughing, back on the same beach, staring at the same burning sun I had just crawled away from. I wanted to scream, but the water in my throat only produced a gurgling sound. My salty tears mixed with the ocean water, and I wasn't sure if I had produced the ocean with my tears or if the ocean had produced me. How was I back here? Surely the waves had carried me. I had to do better.

Frustrated, I gathered the last of the strength in my frail body and rose to my feet. I looked at the ocean in front of me and yelled into the ethers as I charged into the sea. I half staggered, half ran, as I stumbled back into the sea. I ran into the waves and let them consume me again. As I splashed through the waves, I felt the current sweep my legs out from under me as another wave crashed down on my torso, flipping me into the salty froth. I was tossed in a backward somersault, and the back of my neck and head burned as it was dragged harshly through the sand until I was spit back out onto the sandy shore.

This time I lay there for a while trying to regain my composure, but as the hot sun bore down upon me and dried the water from my body, I knew I had to move again. The jungle behind me was not an option, but I had to leave this place for good. I crawled back into the ocean, and once more I was returned in a frazzled heap to the unforgiving beach. I cried out to God. Why he had forsaken me? I had lived with nothing but pain and sorrow. Where was the mercy? I was never promised mercy though. I had taken it upon myself to wander into that jungle, and this is where it had led me. Broken and insane on a beach that led me to a death that awaited me and yet refused to take me. I couldn't lay here and let the sun eat me alive. I'd rather go into the waves.

I crawled in, time and time again with the same result. I was repeatedly spit back out onto the beach. The struggle was impossible. It took my breath, drained my energy, and made me question why I deserved this torture. Death wouldn't take me. Life didn't want me. This beach was torture, an endless purgatory in which the fires of hell were stoked in my soul. I had nothing left. Nothing. I couldn't cry out, and I couldn't cry tears. There was no one there to help, there never was. It was always only me, and given the choice between life and death, I had always chose the latter.

This time death was inevitable, but I refused to surrender my last little bit of control. I didn't want to be consumed by the hot sun, to be wrought with blisters and burns until I was eventually scorched to death by its rays. I'd much rather die in the sea, quick and easy, in minutes... to feel the same sustaining water of life fill my windpipe and lungs and carry me off into oblivion.

I crawled forward again. One hand at a time sinking into, then clawing at, the burning sand I drug my body inch by inch across the beach until I reached the cool wet sand once more. As my fingers dug into the wet sand, a shallow wave filled the small holes my fingers left behind creating small rivulets.

Almost there. This sliver of hope gave me the tiniest push I needed to continue moving forward, to slide off and push myself beneath the next incoming waves and into the depths.

Waves. Waves came and went. Crashing through my grey matter. Soft, gentle forgiving waves. Then harsh, unforgiving waves. They threw my mangled body into a heavy wash cycle, spinning me through the breakers until I was cast back out onto the deathly hot bed of sand. That was it. I was done. There was nothing left. It's not that I wanted to surrender. I had to. I had tried unsuccessfully to rid myself of this life over and over again. I was such a failure that even when I tried to kill myself, I failed disgracefully. So I closed my eyes and drifted off, and surrendered, letting the sun take me.

That's when God reached out to me, not in my language, but in His own unique form. He sent a lone coconut falling from a tree. A ripe coconut filled with the elixir of cool fresh water inside. Life sustaining, thirst quenching, healing nectar. The coconut fell from the tree and into the sand below. It rolled down the small sandy hill right towards my lifeless body until it made contact with my shoulder. The coconut on my shoulder jarred me awake…

My eyes flew open. My soon-to-be wife was looking down at me with her beautiful green eyes as her hand shook my shoulder, rousing me awake, the same shoulder the coconut had just nudged. "Hey baby, wake up. We've got a big day ahead."

I lay frozen for a second until I surrendered to this new reality in front of me. Reality came flooding back to me in waves. *Today is my wedding day.* It was beautiful and magical. I wasn't in some lost world alone anymore. I was in Riviera Maya, Mexico surrounded by family and friends. I'd been coming here for a decade now to both Riviera Maya and Tulum. It had been almost ten years since I first experienced the Mayan Temazcal ceremony in Tulum, an experience that brought my life full circle.

I walked out to the balcony and looked out at the view in front of me. Beyond the palm trees, the ocean stretched out for infinity. I stood mesmerized as the blue waves danced along the shore, pushing and pulling, giving and taking. The water called to me, and the sun was waiting for me. Today, they bring me life. Today I long to play in the waves and the sun's rays, to appreciate the dark jungle behind me. The jungle almost killed me. It ripped me to shreds, yet in the end it gave me strength. It brought me life, and now I was going to surrender to that notion and appreciate every breath and every blessing, every hardship and every bit of sorrow. For now though, I had joy ahead of me. I began to get dressed. A new chapter begins today in a story that never ends. I can't wait to see what happens next.

Made in the USA
Middletown, DE
29 October 2023

41562245R00172